WHY SHOULD

YOU BELIEVE?

A logical foundation for faith

Francis David Batcheler

The cover image is a NASA photograph free from copyright

Acknowledgments

I am grateful to my wife, Rosa, for encouraging me throughout this work and examining it for errors The following people took the time to read the work and offered encouragement, corrections and suggestions for additional information greatly improving the book. Malcolm Eglinton, Dr. Michael Groves, David Meredith David Reed. Geraldine Reid, Claire Reid, Professor David A. Humphreys, Philip Nye, and Edward Shaw.
Any remaining errors are my responsibility.

2nd edition

Francis David Batcheler has a Bachelor of Science in Physics and a Master of Science in Electrical Engineering from the University of Manchester, England. He also holds a Master of Business Administration Degree from Adelphi University, Garden City, New York, USA.

US English Edition

DEDICATED TO

Alyssa, Andrew, Colleen, Rosa.

Why should you believe?

CONTENTS

5

Introduction

When we look at the world around us we find ourselves responding with many emotions. We see magnificent sights such as the Grand Canyon, or a sunset over the ocean and we are filled with awe. When we look at the animal and plant world we see beauty and complexity that naturally point us to a designer. In the past this has led the majority of people to believe in a God who created all things and keeps them in order. The belief in this order was the driving force behind the founders of modern science, such as Sir Isaac Newton, driving him to look for the laws that governed the universe in the sure knowledge that God was sustaining these laws and they would be constant. Even Darwin, who is portrayed by modern atheists as one of them, wrote in the last edition of his book "Origin of the Species," published during his life, that "There is grandeur in this view of life, with its several powers having been originally breathed by the Creator into a few forms or into one....."

There have always been people who did not accept the idea of a God. A Psalm written three thousand years ago said "the fool has said in his heart there is no God" but such people held their beliefs against the evidence of design all around them and in opposition to the beliefs of most of the intellectuals of their time.

Popular culture, often used to have a neutral attitude to religious faith, is now often hostile to Christianity. Television discussion programs allow atheists to attack the idea of God as if science has proved no God exists, whilst authors of fiction often let us know the atheistic views of their heroes, even when they are irrelevant to the story. Recent decades have seen a great reduction in the numbers of people who attend church in the West and an apparent indifference to religion by the majority of the people. At the same time there has been a great increase in crime and an attitude of complete self interest on the part of many people.

In the second World War people in the UK and the USA prayed for victory and peace that came in 1945 and in the post war years large congregations worshipped God, thanking him for their deliverance. The following years have brought prosperity to millions of people in both countries beyond the dreams of previous generations, but instead of resulting in greater worship there has been a decline in meaningful belief in God. What we now see is a culture of selfish materialism that extends throughout all classes of society. There is a widespread belief that our prosperity is due to our own efforts and we deserve all the material goods we can buy. At the same time many people who did not need to lock their doors now live in fear, even when their doors are bolted and there is little concept of the difference between right and wrong. If I can get away with it then it is OK as far as many people are concerned.

This change of belief system is not an accident. Atheists have been waging a war of ideas in which scientific theories are described as fact and false ideas of Christian beliefs are set up as straw men so that they can be knocked down, allowing Christian ideas to be ridiculed. When a political party uses this sort of destructive criticism of their rivals on television in western nations, the opposition parties demand the opportunity to counter the arguments against them, or are allowed to present their point of view at the same time. Atheists have been able in both formal presentations and through expressed opinions of their fictional creations to present their views week after week without any competent rebuttal.

The message of Jesus is, if true, the most important piece of information you will ever read. Jesus declared that all people had fallen short of God's standards and they could not hope to get right with God by their own efforts. Most people are aware that they do not live up to their own standards of good behavior even though today's culture tries to assure us that I'm OK and you're OK whatever we do. Jesus claimed that he had come from God to live a perfect life showing us, by example, what a perfect life looked like. Jesus also claimed that he paid the penalty for all our sins by dying for us. The message of Jesus gives life meaning and purpose, and has been shown to result in people who are more content and live longer. If we were created by God and He loves us there is a meaning to life, but if we are the result of a series of extraordinary accidents the human race with all its achievements will eventually be destroyed and our lives are ultimately pointless.

If the words of Jesus are true we can receive full forgiveness for our sins, together with guidance and peace in our lives by following him. We can also have the certainty that we will spend eternity with God. If there is the possibility that Jesus is right it is worth considering his claims.

The arguments of atheists have changed over time but have included attacks on the reliability of the Bible, on the philosophical idea of God and attacks through the findings of science. All of these attacks have been defended by Christians and Jews who are outstanding authorities in their fields and I refer to many of their works in the following pages. The goal of this book is to show that the objections of atheists are not well founded and to encourage the reader to examine the claims of Christ in the knowledge that the scriptures are reliable and that known science strongly suggests a creator. The reader should then be able to accept the teachings of Jesus, if he or she so chooses, without feeling that they are taking a step of blind faith that has no intellectual justification.

I went to school and university during the 1950s and 1960s, a time when the UK was going through a great change. Sunday schools and churches that were full in the early fifties started the long decline as people began to watch an increasing amount of television on a Sunday. Many television programs allowed atheists to air their beliefs with little opposition. In 1953 a scientist produced amino acids by passing electric currents at high voltages through chemical mixtures that were supposed to simulate liquids found on earth 3 to 4 billion years ago when life was believed to have started. Since amino acids were the building blocks for proteins, popular science led people to believe that life would soon be created artificially from an inorganic mix of chemicals. At the same time physicists put forward their theories of continuous creation, suggesting that the bible was wrong when it taught that there was a start to time and the universe. I had a hard time in the science stream at school defending the faith I was brought up in and found little help from available Christian authors. The book "Why Believe?" that was a general defense of the faith by Rendle Short, who was a surgeon and geologist was some help to me, however. There were also the writings of C.S.Lewis whose logical common sense approach gave me insights then and still refreshes my faith when I read them now.

When I was a physics undergraduate at Manchester University I attended a lecture on Cosmology by Sir Bernard Lovell that was important to me in my search for the truth. Sir Bernard discussed the big bang theory and the theories of Bondi, Gold and Hoyle. He also revealed the new information that his research at Jodrell Bank radio telescope had shown that the radio stars were moving away from us. This supported the big bang theory that I believe to be compatible with the biblical account. About this time the book "The Universe Plan or Accident" by Dr. Robert Clark appeared and supplied a welcome insight into the views of a professional scientist who was also a Christian. During my working life as an electronics development engineer I was fortunate to attend churches in England and the USA whose members included a number of highly qualified scientists, enabling me to keep in touch with their views. I did not have time to develop firm opinions on all the areas where Christians are attacked however, but I determined that as soon as I retired and no longer had to keep up with the fast changing world of electronics I would review the Christian faith together with modern science and come to some conclusions about the strengths and weaknesses of the arguments that are still leveled at Christians. Shortly after I had embarked on this interesting project a chance remark from my son got me thinking that a book explaining my conclusions would be of great help to young Christians or anyone who wishes to honestly examine Christianity. In this era, when scorn is poured on anyone with faith by the atheists who dominate the media, my intention is to show that an intelligent person can embrace the Christian faith. I hope that the book will help those who are seeking for the truth to find it, and enable young Christians to find information with which to defend their faith as I did in "The Universe Plan or Accident"

The novelist Maria Edgeworth was a friend of the great economist David Ricardo about whom she is reported to have said "I never argued or discussed a question with any person who argues more fairly or less for victory and more for the truth." I undertook the study on this book to find the truth for myself and intend that it should be of use to those searching for the truth. I found some of the books I read during the course of the work to be written by people who used debating techniques designed to win their point of view, stretching analogies to breaking point and ignoring facts that did not support them. I hope to have avoided such bias.

Chapter 1

The Reliability of the New Testament

Before we consider the words of Jesus we may want to know the reliability of the New Testament that is our main source of information.

The criticism of the New Testament by atheists has many levels. A few would doubt that we can know anything about Jesus, if he even existed, while others doubt that the words we have recorded are the words that he actually spoke.

Before we examine the New Testament it would help us to know if any non-Christian documents confirm the existence of Jesus. Josephus was a Jewish historian in the first century whose works include a 20 volume set entitled "Antiquities of the Jews." His writings confirm several incidents recorded in the New Testament, including the fact that Jesus performed miraculous acts and that he was crucified by order of Pilate.[1] Later works by Jewish Rabbis also confirm the miracles of Jesus but they ascribe them to sorcery.[2]

The Roman historian Tacitus recording the great fire of Rome says that Nero chose Christians as scapegoats and punished them severely. He goes on to say that Christians got their name from Christus who had been executed by Pontius Pilate.[3]

In the light of these records by non Christian historians of the first century it must be accepted by any reasonable person that Jesus Christ lived, was crucified, and that it was widely held that he performed miraculous acts.

When considering the reliability of the New Testament it is worth making a comparison with other works of a similar age, as Professor Bruce has done at length. A short extract from his work reads "The history of Thucydides (c. 460-400 BC) is known to us from eight manuscripts, the earliest belonging to c. AD 900, and a few papyrus scraps, belonging to about the beginning of the Christian era. The same is true of the History of Herodotus (c. 488-428 BC). Yet no classical scholar would listen to an argument that the authenticity of Herodotus or Thucydides is in doubt..."[4] The New Testament exists in more than 5000 manuscripts and papyri copied between about 130 AD and 350 AD. These include the almost complete Chester Beatty New Testament in three papyri, the earliest of which is from around 200 AD. The veracity of these documents have been the subject of more scholarly research than any other ancient documents, so it is clear that the critics of the authenticity of the New Testament are applying standards that would be regarded as unrealistic if applied to any other document of similar age.

Critics like to debate the authorship and age of the gospels, but the earliest documents in the New Testament are the letters of Paul whose most important doctrinal letters were all written by the year AD. 62, around 30 years after the crucifixion of Jesus and the authorship and approximate date of most of these is beyond dispute. So when Paul says that on one occasion more than 500 people saw Jesus after his resurrection of whom "the majority are still alive"[5,] he left himself open to ridicule if that was anything less than the truth. We could obtain a good idea of the main teaching of Jesus from Paul's letters if we had no other New Testament writings.

Now the letters of Paul were widely circulated around the churches from a very early date because we know that Clement, bishop of Rome, writing to the Corinthian Church in about 96 AD tells them to look at a passage from the letter Paul had written to them in Corinth. He also quotes from Paul's letters to the Romans, Ephesians and Titus.[6] Other quotations in this letter can be traced to the books of the Acts, Hebrews and 1 Peter as well as the Synoptic Gospels. It is clear that the Christians in Rome already had copies of several of Paul's letters even at this early date. All the other churches would desire copies of Paul's letters and in the age of Roman rule, when travel was safe and common, many copies were made and distributed widely.

Paul describes how he persecuted the church in its early days and was brought to conversion by a miraculous intervention by the resurrected Jesus, that was so convincing to him that he was prepared to be beaten, stoned and finally put to death, rather than renounce his faith in the risen Jesus.[7] He was clearly a man of great integrity, who described himself as the greatest of sinners for his part in the persecution of the church and none of the criticisms of Paul suggest that he was dishonest in his writings.

Paul wrote his letters to churches or individuals who needed correction or guidance. They were probably acquainted with the main facts about the life of Jesus so Paul only mentions them when they are relevant to his message. So we learn about the crucifixion and resurrection of Jesus and about his instructions for the communion remembrance service, but we learn nothing of the method of Jesus' teaching using illustrative stories, nor the details of his travels that we find in the gospels. What we do get is the gospel message in Paul's own words and his instructions concerning how the Christian life should be lived day by day. Some authors have suggested that Paul distorted the teachings of Jesus or even that he invented Christianity, but a comparison with the Gospels shows that his teachings agreed with those of Jesus on all the main areas that both expounded.

The defining message of Jesus as expressed by his disciple John is: "For God loved the world so much that he gave his only Son that everyone who believes on him should not be lost but have eternal life."[8] Paul expresses it as follows," everyone has sinned, everyone falls short of the beauty of God's plan. Under this divine system *anyone* who has faith is now freely acquitted in the eyes of God by his generous dealing in the redemptive act of Jesus Christ."[9] We can see that Paul was preaching the same message as Jesus, a fact that the apostle Peter, who spent three years under instruction from Jesus, must have believed when he tells the readers of his second letter to look at the teachings of Paul.[10]

Atheists and liberal theologians sometimes suggest that we do not know who wrote the gospels because we do not have the assurance we have in the writings of Paul where he clearly identifies each letter with his name. We do have strong circumstantial evidence, however, that the gospel of Luke and the book of Acts were written by Luke and that the gospel of John was written by John the disciple of Jesus, from a careful reading of the gospel and Paul's letters.

Papias, a bishop of Hierapolis, wrote some of his recollections of discussions he had with a number of disciples of the apostles and possibly the apostle John himself. He wrote five books in about 115 AD but only fragments of them exist today. Quotations from his books by later authors say that Matthew wrote the Logia in Aramaic and that Mark wrote his Gospel from the preaching of Peter while they were both in Rome. The Logia is believed to be a collection of the sayings of Jesus in the language that Jesus used and linguists say that they can detect the underlying Aramaic in Matthew's Gospel. There will always be some dispute amongst historians about the authorship of the Gospels but it is beyond the scope of this book to pursue all the arguments in depth.

We will now look at the writings of Luke author of both the Gospel of Luke and the book of Acts. I intend to show that the writings of Luke have been subject to considerable scrutiny and proved to be accurate, allowing us to study them with confidence in their reliability. Luke was a Greek, the only non-Jewish author that we know of in the Bible. He wrote with the precision of an educated Greek, specifying times, where possible, with reference to one or more important people or events. For example, he specifies the date when John the Baptist began to preach with the words "In the fifteenth year of the reign of the Emperor Tiberius (a year when Pontius Pilate was governor of Judea, Herod tetrarch of Galilee, his brother Philip tetrarch of the territory of Ituraea and Trachonitis and Lysanias as the tetrarch of Abilene while Annas and Caiaphas were the High Priests)"[11] To describe a time with such detail required research (and Luke did not have the Internet to help him), but Luke, as we will show, was careful to be accurate in all his writings. The first verses of Luke explain why he is writing this book and introduce us to the most excellent Theophilus who is to get the first copy. Luke was a Greek convert who traveled with Paul on some of his missionary journeys and he tells Theophilus that, although he knew many other people had written accounts of the ministry of Jesus, he had decided to present the facts on which the Gospel was based in their "proper order" so that Theophilus would have "reliable information."[12] Now we know that Luke was in Rome at the same time as Mark because Paul records an occasion when both Mark, the cousin of Barnabas, and Luke, the beloved doctor, were visiting him in a Roman jail.[13] There is also evidence that Mark wrote his gospel in Rome using the preaching of Peter as his source.[14] Luke clearly made use of this same opportunity to get the facts from Peter. More than half the verses in the Gospel of Mark appear with little change in the Gospel of Luke, but Luke used other sources as well to produce the longest of the Gospels.

To illustrate the care that Luke took in his writing we will examine his second book, the Acts of the Apostles, that was also written as a letter to Theophilus. This is an account of how the church spread after the risen Jesus had appeared to his followers, who were despondent and scattered after his death. In this book we have several passages where Luke includes himself in the proceedings. For example Acts chapter 20 verse 13 says "Meanwhile we had gone aboard the ship and sailed on ahead for Assos, intending to pick up Paul there," Clearly Luke was present for part of the missionary journeys and had time to talk to some of the Apostles to ascertain all the facts. Paul and his associates traveled from town to town preaching the Gospel, often coming into conflict with the governing authority. The correct titles of these local dignitaries were many and varied and they were changed from time to time by the authorities in Rome. As Professor Bruce points out, Cyprus was an imperial province governed by an imperial legate until 22 BC when it became a senatorial province governed by a proconsul, as stated by Luke.[15] Luke's history follows the missionary group through town after town, detailing the titles of the authorities the missionaries dealt with, including the title of "politarchs" for the magistrates in Thessalonica, a title not found in classical literature.[16] These details could not be checked by historians in Victorian times, that led to a belief that the book of Acts was filled with errors.

The archaeologist Sir William Ramsey was skeptical about the accuracy of Acts and set out to find the truth and discredit the writings of Luke and thereby discredit the New Testament once and for all. In fact every detail of Luke was found to be correct, even down to finding the obscure title of "politarch" on an ancient inscription. Ramsey concluded his investigations with the words "I set out to look for the truth on the borderland where Greece and Asia meet and found it there (in the book of Acts). You may press the words of Luke in a degree beyond any historian's and they stand the keenest scrutiny and the hardest treatment...."[17]

It is hard to imagine that Luke would take so much care about the details of Acts and take less care about his Gospel, remembering that when he released his work to the "most excellent Theophilus" it would be easily possible for his work to be checked. Luke used the term "most excellent" to describe local governors like Felix[18] and although the position of Theophilus is not known, if he were a man of authority it would be an extra reason for Luke to double check any statements he made.

Now at this point you may say that there is a good possibility that what Luke wrote was accurate, but how do we know that the New Testament we have is what the authors put down? In the first century Christianity spread very widely through the world with active churches in Rome, Asia Minor, Egypt and to the east of the Roman Empire into the Parthian Empire where the Jews had long established communities. All of these groups had the gospels and the letters of Paul and they made translations into several languages during the first three centuries. Although we have no record of the missionary journeys of the Christians in the Parthian Empire, we know they took the gospel message through to western China. We also have the report of a Christian traveler in India around 180 AD confirming that they had a copy of the Gospel of Matthew before he arrived.[19] The many translations included copying errors, additions and omissions and when the church became accepted in the Roman Empire, during the fourth century, the need for a single accepted text was realized. This text was called the Byzantium text after Byzantium (now Istanbul) that was at the time the Imperial capital and became the standard (or received) text that provided the source for the English Authorized Version of King James.

Now this is all very well but how do we know if the Byzantine text is an accurate representation of the autograph script? This is where the 5000 early documents are of such value because it has been possible to catergorize them into groups with common characteristics. Scholars have identified Alexandrian, Ceasarean, Western (mainly Roman) and Syriac texts. Different English translations have been completed from these families of early documents. The Revised Version of 1881 and the American Standard Version of 1901 used the Alexandrian Text as the main source. The Revised Standard Version of 1946, together with the New International Version of 1983, are the work of scholars who considered all the documents on their merits and believed they have achieved a translation that represents the wording of the second century documents.[20]

When considering the variations in the available documents, the editors of The New King James Version of 1992 state in their preface "Readers may be assured that the textual debate does not affect one word in a thousand words of the Greek New Testament. Furthermore no established doctrine is called into question by any doubts about the correct reading of this or that text."

Television commentators may cast doubts about the accuracy of the Bible but the serious seeker after truth should take note of the words of one of the most notable scholars of New Testament textual criticism: "The interval then between the dates of original composition and the earliest extant evidence becomes so small as to be in fact negligible, and the last foundation for any doubt that the Scriptures have come down to us substantially as they were written has now been removed. Both the *authenticity* and the *general integrity* of the books of the New Testament may be regarded as finally established."[21]

Chapter 2

Evidence for God

When Jesus raised Lazarus from the dead he had been buried for several days and he came out of the tomb still wrapped in his burial garments. Jesus was approaching the end of his time on earth and he said the raising of Lazarus was a miracle performed as a sign, so that those around might believe.[1] The result was that many did believe, but some went and told the enemies of Jesus what they had seen, to warn them of the need to act quickly to get rid of him, before he had too many followers. If a resurrection from the dead is insufficient to persuade some people of the power of God, it is not going to be possible for God to convince them of his existence unless he picks them up and shakes them. This action would of course remove their doubts but would also remove their free will.

It is clear that many authors of the Old Testament expected mankind to look at the obvious signs of design in nature and deduce from that the existence of a designer.[2] This connection between nature and God was questioned by philosophers in the eighteenth century and further called into doubt by the work of Darwin. In the nineteenth century William Paley argued that if he found a watch lying on a field he would be forced to the conclusion that it owed its existence to a watchmaker who had skillfully constructed the watch piece by piece and assembled the various pieces with precision, to ensure that it worked as designed.[3] He extrapolated this argument to the animal kingdom concluding that the ability of animals to perform many complex functions showed evidence of design that pointed to a designer.

This argument has been attacked on the basis of the difference between an inanimate object that clearly can do nothing to alter its state and a living organism that may have the ability to adapt. This argument predates Darwin, but Darwin's theory that animal development took place in a series of very small changes, caused by random mutations, that could become permanent changes only if they gave the animal a survival advantage, was seized on by atheists as an argument against the existence of God. Darwin saw his theory as providing a mechanism whereby God created the animal kingdom as shown by this quotation from the last edition of Origin of the Species published in his lifetime: "There is a grandeur in this view of life, with its several powers having been originally breathed by the Creator into a few forms or into one and........from so simple a beginning endless forms so beautiful and most wonderful have been and are being evolved."[4] Atheists saw Darwin's theory as providing an alternative to God as an explanation for the complexities of design seen in nature and for this reason they have clung to Darwinism with religious fervor, at times providing false scientific evidence for evolution and even misquoting Darwin to eliminate the word "Creator" in his work.[5]

The discoveries of microbiology have revealed microsystems in living things whose development without external aid is difficult to conceive. Michael Behe[6] suggests that evolution by gradual improvement cannot apply to complex subsystems made up of interacting parts that provide no survival advantage to the animal individually, but work together to provide a vital function. Behe describes several such systems, that he calls irreducibly complex, comparing them to the simple mousetrap having five components. These components are of no use whatsoever unless all five are made with sufficient precision and assembled correctly. The designer who made three of these components would not have a mousetrap working at 60% efficiency, he would have nothing of value at all. An animal in whom random mutations had produced three of the five components of a useful working system would not have its survival enhanced by them and by Darwin's theories either they or the animal would not survive. The issue of evolution and faith will be considered further in Chapter 5, so in this chapter we will look at other reasons why the majority of the world's people believe in God.

Almost all people have a deep acknowledgment that some actions are wrong, they have an inbuilt conscience that tells them when they are doing wrong. At the time I am writing this there are television programs running in the USA and Britain called "The Apprentice." The idea is that a number of capable young people are given the opportunity to perform various tasks set by a wealthy business person, who eliminates the ones who perform badly. The contestant who has completed the tasks most satisfactorily is offered a well paying job. The tasks often involve persuading potential customers to buy products or potential suppliers to sell at a discount. The persuasive methods used by the contestants sometimes involve blatant lies. Often when defending their performance in the meetings with the entrepreneur after each task, the truth is once again stretched. The British contestants who lose week by week are subsequently interviewed by another panel who analyze their performance. This program highlights the lack of honesty in the contestants and they respond in various ways. Some suggest that their actions were misunderstood, while some are embarrassed at being found out, clearly realizing they have ignored their conscience. A third group imply that it is necessary to lie to get results. There is a fundamental understanding in virtually all contestants that lying is wrong, but some of them clearly think that doing wrong is justified if it brings them benefits. One or two contestants had so numbed their conscience that they hardly knew they were lying, but they usually recognized it when it was pointed out to them.

C.S.Lewis suggested that there exists a "moral law" and his research revealed that there was a great deal of agreement among different peoples around the world about the main planks of this standard, by which people judge decent behavior.[7] He argued that this is not the instinct for self survival, indeed we often need to choose between conflicting instincts. Some years ago I attended a church where the pastor was a surgeon at a local hospital. When he retired, a column was written about him in a national newspaper and it was revealed that he had the highest medal for gallantry that Britain awards to civilians. During the second world war a bomb destroyed part of the hospital where he was working and a nurse was trapped under the rubble. The pile of rubble was unsafe and his first instinct must have been to get out of the building to safety, but instead he crawled under the rubble and saved the nurse's life. Although we understand the first reaction, there are few if any societies on earth who would not admire the selfless action he took and regard the safe option as cowardly. When we accept that selfless actions are superior to selfish actions we are acknowledging the existence of a moral law. This law results in behavior that may be contrary to the behavior we would expect from the law of "the survival of the fittest."

A recent film (Schindler's List) told the true story of a German who risked his life in Nazi Germany saving the lives of Jews while it was the policy of his Government to murder the entire Jewish population of Europe. There was no apparent positive outcome of this action for him, as the German military was extremely powerful and he could not know that Russia, the British Empire and the USA would combine to defeat it. He was not being loyal to the government of his country or obeying his instinct for self preservation, he simply did what he believed was right day after day, in the knowledge that he could face the fate from which he was saving others. At the end of that war many Germans who committed atrocities excused themselves by saying they were only obeying orders, acknowledging that what they did was wrong, but Schindler disobeyed the laws of his country to do what he believed was right and has received almost universal commendation for his brave actions. There are countless cases where men and women have taken similar heroic actions for people they did not even know whilst others have followed their instinct for self survival. It is clear that the moral law is not just instinct because, as C.S Lewis says, we often have to choose between instincts, and one instinct is not necessarily the right one under all conditions. We may not always follow this moral law but very few people do not recognize its superiority.

The Roman church recently had problems because some members of its clergy were molesting children. It had to balance the conflicting instincts of showing mercy or demanding justice and it was felt that as a church showing mercy should be paramount. This allowed the offenders to continue their activities and was clearly the wrong decision. The rights of the victims to be protected was clearly more important than showing mercy to the criminal and when it became public that the wrong choice had been made there was universal condemnation for the actions of the leaders of the church, followed by acknowledgment by them of their error. When we consider generosity against miserliness, courage against cowardliness, helping the needy against stealing from the helpless, all normal people know which is right without having lessons in ethics; but we all know that we don't always live up to our own standards of behavior.

It is possible to distort the moral code of course. Recently a paedophile was interviewed on BBC television[8] and refused to agree with the interviewer that sex with children was wrong. The interviewer (whose religious faith is unknown to the author) simply did not know what to say next. She was assuming that all people would agree on this basic standard of decent behavior, but this man lived with his indecency, by denying it was wrong and as a result the interviewer had no common ground on which to start a reasonable discussion.

Many peoples in history have recognized this absolute standard of goodness and realized that they did not live up to it. They often believed that in breaking this code they were offending their God (or Gods) and devised methods aimed at appeasing them. Many religious people believe that they should try to have their good works outnumber their bad, or follow a routine that will please God in the hope that the balance will be all right in the end. It is difficult to understand why people who became aware of their sins should invent an all powerful God who demands that they should live a sinless life. Of course some peoples such as the Greeks devised Gods who were capricious in their actions and showed little interest in the behavior of humans. It was the Jews who claimed to have prophets dealing directly with God. These prophets revealed that God wanted people to avoid sinful behavior because he cared for them. Some of the earliest writings in Genesis show God's anger at sexual immorality and idolatry. It is difficult to understand why anyone would invent an all powerful God who demanded perfection unless they wanted to use this knowledge to exploit the populace. However the evidence of the Old Testament is that the prophets who instructed the Jews on the standards God expected were often persecuted for their troubles and it was the Kings and rulers who flouted the prophet's teaching and abused their power.

Religious people have for many centuries believed that God has given them a basic conscience but atheists are leading people to believe that there is no absolute standard, and this leads many to the conclusion that the only thing that matters is getting what you want for yourself now. Many atheists want to pick and choose between the laws of God. The prosperous atheists who write books promoting their cause are keen to acknowledge their support for selective parts of the moral code. They usually uphold property laws whilst they may decide to ignore God's teaching on fidelity in marriage. Not surprisingly the population who embrace atheism, or choose to ignore God, feel free to make their own choice about which moral laws they will accept and many now consider excessive drinking and sexual immorality to be normal behavior. The resulting disease and unwanted children are regarded by atheistic governments as the result of poor education, when the lack of absolute standards is the real cause. It is not surprising that the contestants on The Apprentice lie to try to gain an advantage for themselves in this Godless culture where everyone makes up their own rules. It is still true, however, that most of the contestants are conscious of the moral law that God has built into them and show some shame when their deceptions are pointed out.

So far we have looked at the evidence of God in the moral code that he has built into our consciousness. Now I would like to highlight the appreciation of beauty in art and music as inbuilt gifts of God. There are a number of people who have the disability of being tone deaf. In almost all conditions of life they are at no survival disadvantage compared with someone with perfect pitch. Similarly people with no appreciation of art lead successful lives. Indeed it could be argued that for people struggling to earn the basic necessities of life, any nonproductive distraction such as learning to play an instrument or taking time to paint could lead to an early death. There have been examples of artists who were unable to make a living from their art and died in poverty following their muse, making it difficult to argue that the love of art contributed to their survival, but early drawings on cave walls show this gift was present in mankind when survival must have been a continual struggle. The word "gift" in relation to the outstanding artistic talents implies a giver. There is a video that is often televised of the Berlin Philharmonic accompanying a young violin virtuoso that illustrates this idea. As the young woman plays she is watched with obvious admiration by the first violins who are much older than her and very capable players, but they know that however hard they work they simply do not have the talent that this girl has. The virtuoso was born with a God-given ability that most people cannot achieve however hard they work.

The gift of a sense of humor would seem to be far from essential for survival but is understandable as a gift from God to improve our lives. It is not difficult to imagine a twinkle in the eyes of Jesus when he said it was harder for a rich man to get into the kingdom of heaven than for a camel to pass through the eye of a needle. (Of course it is difficult for anyone to get into the kingdom of heaven but as we shall see Jesus made the way straightforward for us.)

The atheist's view of the world is necessarily tied up with the idea of the survival of the fittest. There is no doubt how that should work in modern society. The sales director of a company where I was employed had very definite ideas about what was wrong with modern life. He used the example of the American pioneers who pushed into the unknown and were completely self sufficient. He argued against any free health care, believing that only those who had earned enough to pay for treatment should get it. His opinion about aid to developing countries was equally hard. He argued that the USA and Europe made it on their own, and if other countries were unable to do so they should be allowed to starve. This viewpoint, that is surely the natural outcome of a belief in evolution as the only reason for life, would result in more for the successful, whilst ensuring that the world does not get overcrowded as the unsuccessful would die. Few people would accept this philosophy openly and politicians are keen to demonstrate how generous they are with overseas aid, using taxpayer's money. But how could the idea of helping remote strangers appear in brains that have developed under the evolutionary pressures of survival of the fittest?

A final pointer to God is found in the multitude of men and women who have felt called by God to perform a specified task and who have known the presence of God with them when apparently impossible obstacles were removed. Amongst the women who stepped into the unknown, Gladys Aylward felt she was being led to go to China as a missionary but was unable to get any support from missionary societies.[9] With little money or knowledge of the language she traveled to China and spent a lifetime seeing God at work there. When the Japanese attacked China she led a large group of children to safety on a treacherous mountain trail. Gladys Aylward became very well known and a Hollywood film was made dramatizing her life story. I heard Gladys describe her true story that lacked the glamour and romance that Hollywood had added but told of a life in which God had provided for her in desperate and dangerous circumstances.

The Christian faith is essentially a practical faith in which we are told to follow where God leads and that he will provide the resources. No example illustrates this more than the life of George Muller[10] because he took such care to record his experiences. In 1830 George Muller was a minister in the small town of Teignmouth in the south of England. His income came from "pew fees" that his congregation were charged for their seats in the church. George came to the conclusion that this was a fee for hearing the gospel and he decided that this was not in keeping with God's will that the gospel should be freely available to all so, after much prayer, he discontinued these charges. He chose instead to leave a box at the back of the church into which free will offerings could be placed to support him. It is important to note that he decided that he would not tell any individual about the state of his finances, but if he were put in the position where he would be forced to go into debt to survive he would reconsider his decision. He also kept accurate records of the money and gifts he received. On many occasions he was almost without funds to pay the rent or buy food for the next meal, but on every occasion his needs were met, often just in time. Within weeks of abolishing pew fees his resolve was tested and he was almost bankrupt. On the day he would have been forced to admit defeat, a church member he was visiting said she had been prompted by the Lord to give him 42 shillings. He records many situations where his faith was tested to the last minute. On a Sunday evening in November 1831 he had only 2 1/2 pence left and a little butter. The shops were closed so he would have been unable to buy food if he had money, so he prayed for food for his evening meal. As he was in prayer a member of his congregation called and gave him a large loaf and 5 shillings. Once again his family's needs had been provided for at the last minute.

In 1832 Muller moved to a new church in the city of Bristol where he continued to depend on free will gifts. In that year a cholera epidemic was sweeping through the country, resulting in more than 20,000 deaths. As a result many newly orphaned children joined the ranks of those already living on the streets of all the major cities in Britain. Muller became convinced that he was being called to do something for these children and he organized a meeting of church members to explain what he wanted to do. He purposefully avoided appealing to the audience's emotions and refused to take a collection, intending that his proposals be prayerfully considered. He made it clear that his motives were to help the children, but also to show that God would ensure that his work would get the resources it required if he stepped out in faith. After the meeting a woman offered to help and the next day Muller received a letter from a couple who said they would work full time at the orphanage. They would work without salary, living by faith as Muller did, offering their own furniture for use at the orphanage. Several other offers of help were received together with financial support and on April 21st 1836 Muller opened the rented house where he had been living, 6,Wilson Street, as the home for 32 orphaned girls aged from 7 to 11. It was soon apparent however that many younger children also needed help so Muller rented a second house, 1,Wilson Street, that on November the 28th 1836 opened its doors to infants.

At this time the government had established the workhouse as a place of last resort for the destitute. The dreadful conditions experienced by children in these institutions was later brought to the public's attention by the author Charles Dickens in his classic novel Oliver Twist. In the workhouse children could be forced to work for up to 100 hours per week for a subsistence diet and a bed for the night. Many would run away as Oliver did in the Dickens' novel, preferring the relative freedom of begging on the streets.

Muller now experienced the same "just in time" provision for the children that he and his family had lived by since he abolished pew rents. There are many entries in his notes, such as, "today we have no funds to buy the orphans bread for tea" and "today we have only 2 pence left," but on every occasion food and money was provided and the orphans never missed a meal. Muller now started to pray for the Lord's leading for premises in which to open an orphanage for boys. His prayers were answered and he was soon able to provide a home for orphaned boys in yet another rented property on Wilson street.

In 1841 Muller postponed his annual general meeting because the orphanage had no funds and he felt that to reveal this to the general public would be tantamount to making a general appeal for support and he believed that God should provide for work done in His name. By May 1842 Muller felt the orphanage was in a position of sufficient financial strength for him to let the meeting take place, revealing their financial position without it being regarded as an appeal. This illustrates the steps Muller took to ensure that the work was supported by people who were moved to give by God, not pressured into giving by him making appeals for help.

On the 30th of October 1845 the residents of Wilson Street sent a formal letter to Muller complaining about the noise the orphans made, and the strain on the drains caused by the presence of 150 extra children in what was a residential street. The children's playtimes had been staggered so that the noise was almost continuous, and the drains had suffered several blockages. Muller knew that there were many more children needing places in the orphanage so he began looking for a building to rent that would accommodate 300 children, but without success. He eventually came to the conclusion that he would need to find land and build an orphanage designed for 300 children. The amount of money required would be far larger than the amount received so far, as often they were down to a few pence, so it required great faith to believe that God would provide the thousands of pounds a new building of adequate size would cost. George prayed about the need, then called a meeting of his church and told them of his plans. For the next 36 days he continued praying without response, then on December the 10th 1845 he received his first donation of 1000 pounds for the building of the new orphanage. This was the largest single donation he had ever received. Within a month a second 1000 pounds had been received and Muller's sister-in-law had met an architect in London who volunteered to draw up the plans for the new building and to oversee its construction free of charge.

George found an available piece of land just outside Bristol, a location he thought would be better for the health of the children than breathing the smoky air in the city. He secured a meeting with the land's owner who told him he had been awake from 3 am that morning, tossing and turning in bed, and he had decided to greatly reduce the price of the land. Muller secured seven acres of prime hilltop land for 840 pounds instead of the market price of 1400 pounds. By the end of 1846 the building fund had reached 9000 pounds (about 660,000 pounds or $1million US in 2009 prices) and the foundation stone for the new building was laid in August 1847. By January 1870 five orphanages had been built on the hilltop site and a total of 2000 children could now be accommodated. This massive undertaking was still financed on a day to day basis, still on occasion without any food for the next meal, but every need was always met on time. It was said that it was impossible to defend the atheist position in Bristol because everyone knew what faith had accomplished there.

All the children were provided with three sets of clothing and were taught to read and study. Before the young people left the orphanage a job or apprenticeship had been found for them and they left with three sets of clothes, a Bible and sufficient money to travel to their new employer plus a small amount to sustain them until they were paid.

When George Muller died at the age of 93 the orphanage had looked after more than 10,000 children and well over a million pounds had been given to him to spend on the orphanage and in promotion of the Bible. This would be around 100 million pounds ($160 million US dollars 2009). Charities today advertise on television and in newspapers making national appeals to audiences far larger than the total population of Britain in the nineteenth century, often with full time fund raisers and celebrities. Many of these fail to achieve results equal to those George Muller obtained by prayer and faith.

Today missionaries are urged to get all their financial support in place before they leave for the mission field, unlike many missionaries in the past who went out in faith and told thousands of true stories of God's guidance and support day by day. I have at my side a book by a little known missionary called G.H.Lang[11] who lived by faith for decades in India, often completely running out of money but having sufficient provided just as it was needed. The stories in his book are remarkable examples of God providing for a man obeying his leading. Lang recounts one incident when he was in Egypt without any money, a fact that he had not shared with any other person, but his need was the subject of his prayers. In answer to his prayer he was given a gift of five gold sovereigns that allowed him to complete his journey home. He comments "It is a pity to be a millionaire and for such sweet experiences to be impossible."

A more recent example of faith in action was told to me by Keith Danby. In 1990 Keith lived in the city of Carlisle in the north of England close to an Indian Surgeon called Stephen Alfred. When Stephen left India he was determined not to return, except to visit his family, because he wanted to get away from the corruption that he had experienced in that land. He was tired of the continual need to resort to bribery to get things done. He occupied the position of post-fellowship registrar at Carlisle's main hospital and was becoming an expert in the then new discipline of keyhole surgery. Although in his early 30s Stephen had established an excellent reputation and was expected to have a brilliant career. In the spring of 1990 Stephen believed that God called him to return to India and provide free medical care for some of the poorest people in the world, close to the city of Mumbai. The morning after God spoke to Stephen he visited his friend Keith Danby to discuss it with him and Keith called some friends who established a trust to finance the work. This group of friends assembled some essential equipment and in April 1992 Stephen returned to India to start a new hospital. By the summer of 1998 Stephen was running a 35 bed hospital with a mixture of about 50% paying patients and 50% for whom treatment was free. He supplemented his income by working part time in a city hospital, usually in the mornings, leaving the afternoons and evenings for his new enterprise. By 2001 the hospital had been adopted by Samaritan's Purse, an international relief agency, and had 50 beds including a six bed intensive care unit and a four bed neo-natal unit. It also has optical and dental units and a well equipped pharmacy. In 2010 a new building was opened doubling the number of hospital beds and providing facilities for AIDS patients. Christian medical staff from the West take short term posts in this bustling modern hospital that is the result of a doctor following the leading of God.[12]

Aylward, Muller, Lang and Alfred would find a book on the existence of God unnecessary because they trusted their lives to him and they experienced his provision for themselves.

Richard Dawkins appeared on a recent TV program promoting atheism. He asked a Christian headmaster whether he thought he would be a rapist if he was not a Christian. This appears to be a favorite debate-winning point of Dawkins; if the answer is yes he concludes that you are not someone he would like to know. If it is no he concludes that you don't need saving. I suspect very few people want to commit rape or rob a bank but I have come across a number of Christians who were leading lives of crime before they were saved. Some converts have written books to illustrate how their lives were transformed after conversion. Among the many books written by Christians whose lives were turned from criminal activity "the Cross and the Switchblade"[13] tells the story of a former New York gangmember, and "Once an Arafat Man"[14] chronicles the life change of a former assassin. A powerful example is the life of John Newton, the author of the hymn "Amazing Grace". Newton was a slave trader when he was converted but he came to realize that what he was doing was against the teaching of the bible. It is easy to look back and say that slavery was obviously wrong but it was not at all obvious to people back then. Newton became a church minister and helped Wilberforce and the Christian community to get Parliament to abolish slavery from the British Empire despite considerable opposition. The people who experience life changes like this do not need convincing of the power of God. They have tested the admonition to "taste and see that the Lord is good" and found it to be true.

As Professor Dawkins well knows, it is not just the major sins that define us. During my time in industry there were many occasions when I witnessed dishonesty. On one typical occasion I was in a meeting in the office of a sales director, a cultured university graduate with many years' experience. The meeting was interrupted by a customer on the telephone inquiring about the equipment we were making for him. The director assured him that it was on schedule. As soon as he had finished the call he called the planning department and asked for the status of the project. We then continued the meeting as if nothing had happened. Lies like that are completely accepted in the atheist world. In contrast a professing Christian I know resigned rather than lie to his customer about a delivery date as the top management of his company were demanding.

In case you think that this dishonesty is only in the commercial world, I should add that on two occasions I have had my original work plagiarized, once in a research paper and once in a patent. I am sure there are many other instances when this sort of thing has occurred. When we stop believing in God's law we become our own God and we decide what is right and wrong, that for most people becomes a very flexible guide depending on circumstance and self interest.

This chapter has shown several ways in which we can see evidence of an active creator, both in the way we are made and the way God provides for those who trust him to support them in carrying out a mission for him.

Chapter 3

The Teachings of Jesus

The Christian faith rests on the New Testament record of Jesus that tells of his teachings, his life, his crucifixion and his resurrection. The first thing to notice is that Jesus claimed that he was equal with God in such expressions as "he who has seen me has seen the Father"[1] and "I and my Father are one."[2] These statements cannot be regarded as the words of just a good, sane man.[3] The claim to be equal with God was clearly intended to ensure that his words were to be regarded as of vital importance. When he said "I am the way the truth and the life, no one comes to the Father except through me"[4] he was claiming to speak with divine authority. Millions of people have spent their entire lives following his teachings and for many the result has been persecution and death. Jesus clearly told his disciples that he would be crucified because of his teachings and that they could expect similar treatment if they continued with his work after he had gone.[5] To put these close friends through such a fate if he knew that his teachings were without foundation would be evil, or the act of a mad man. The fact that Jesus was put to death at the instigation of the Jewish authorities makes it clear that they understood the nature of this claim of equality with God and regarded it as blasphemy.[6] The Jewish leaders were quite able to allow a degree of disagreement amongst themselves, as indicated by the apparently wide schism over such a fundamental question as resurrection that the Pharisees accepted and the Sadducees did not. They had also tolerated the teachings of John the Baptist who called them a "brood of vipers"[7] without taking action against him. But John was appealing to the Mosaic law and they could apparently deal with the variation in interpretation that he gave, whereas Jesus said "you have heard that it was said......but I say to you,"[8] claiming to have the authority to interpret scripture in a new way, or to teach completely new revelations. The picture of Jesus that we see in the Bible is of a man whose character and life were in accord with his teachings, but whose claim to have divine authority was too much for the religious leaders to tolerate.

When we study Jesus in the gospels we are faced with the story of a man who could face devious and difficult questions and give well thought out answers in a direct and positive way, showing him to be completely sane. He also healed many people, not in the mode of modern faith healers, where an occasional success is used as a proof, but healing all that came to him in faith,[9] even on occasion healing at a distance.[10] These stories often feel like eye witness accounts in which honesty shines through. What could the apostle John make of Jesus spitting on the ground to make a paste to put on the eyes of a blind man which, when he had washed it off, resulted in a complete cure?[11] John knew that Jesus did not need to make the paste to perform the miracle, but perhaps the blind man needed that procedure to be followed to enhance his faith. The temptation for John to leave that miracle out of his gospel must have been great, but the fact that it included speaks of a reporter who recorded what he saw even when he did not have an explanation for the method used.

The same honesty can be seen in some of the stories told about the early disciples that showed them in a bad light. How easy it would have been to leave out the argument between two disciples about who should be greatest in the kingdom of heaven,[12] or to forget about the skepticism of doubting Thomas.[13] Even more surprising is the inclusion of several accounts of less than ideal behavior by Peter who by the time the gospels were written had certainly been a major force in evangelizing the Roman empire and had probably suffered martyrdom before the gospels of Matthew and John were written. It is a commendably honest author who includes the incidents where Peter lost his faith while walking on the water,[14] received a strong rebuke from Jesus[15] and denied that he was even a disciple.[16]

When explaining the love God has for his people, Jesus told the story of the Prodigal Son. In this a father is portrayed as having two sons and the younger one approached him to ask him for his inheritance before the father dies. This would be deeply painful for any normal father but this loving father agreed to the request, allowing his son to depart, probably with one third of his wealth, that the son promptly wasted on riotous and immoral living. When the money was spent he looked for a job and the only one he could find was tending pigs. The son was so hungry that he was almost prepared to eat the slop that he was feeding to the pigs, but he realized that his father's servants had plenty to eat so he resolved to seek a servant's position with his father. Now many fathers would completely disown their sons at this point and even today we find parents from some societies who will go as far as murdering their children, if they feel they have dishonored the family name. Many of the parents in Jesus' audience must have felt the prodigal son was about to get the humiliation that he deserved, but Jesus told them the father was watching the road to his home, constantly waiting for his son's return.[17] This was the picture that Jesus gave of the love of God and he claimed to know this for a fact. It is a picture of a God who loves you and is ready to forgive your sins and mine, but how can such a God also be Just? There must be a penalty paid for sin.

In the Old Testament the Jewish people were given the privilege of having God reveal himself to them through prophets and he instituted a sin offering in which a young bullock was sacrificed for the acknowledged sins of the people.[18] It was explained to them that this was symbolic, pointing forward to when the Messiah would come to earth and he would be sacrificed for the sins of the world, completely paying the penalty so that no more sin offerings would be required. So Isaiah prophesied the death of Jesus hundreds of years before he was born, explaining it with the words "But he was pierced for our transgressions, he was crushed for our iniquities: the punishment that brought us peace was upon him, and by his wounds we are healed."[19]

Jesus claimed that he was the one spoken about in these verses[20] and that he had come to pay the penalty for your sins and mine. He also claimed to be one with God. So we are faced with the remarkable situation that the God who is demanding righteousness and insisting that there must be a penalty paid for our sins is himself, in the person of Jesus, prepared to take that punishment so that we, who have no means to pay ourselves, might be forgiven freely. What this shows us is how seriously God takes sin, that is in essence a rebellion against him and is directly responsible for the majority of human suffering in this world. Secondly, we learn from the sacrifice of Jesus just how much we are loved by God. Jesus said that "God loved the world so much that he gave his only Son so that everyone who believes in him should not be lost but should have eternal life........Whoever believes in him is not judged at all. It is the one who will not believe who stands condemned already.........This is the judgement-that light has come into the world and men have preferred darkness to light because their deeds are evil."[21]

So all that you have to do for salvation is to acknowledge that you are a sinner, you do not even meet your own standards much less God's. Then accept that Jesus died to pay the penalty for your sins and ask him to come into your life and save you. It is often claimed that this salvation gives us perfect freedom, meaning that we no longer have to strive to get right with God the way many religions try to do. Of course you need to read the New Testament and see how God wants you to behave, but many of the urges that drive people to destructive lifestyles will fade away because you will have the presence of the Holy Spirit guiding you towards constructive goals for your life.

It is important to note that Jesus taught that he was returning to his Father to prepare a place for those who follow him, but those who choose to reject him will find themselves separated from God for eternity and denied access to heaven.[22,23] This may seem rather harsh, but when you look around this world where we have been allowed the freedom to choose the moral code we will follow, we see how our choices would make heaven just like today's world. God clearly wants heaven to be a much better place where everyone is committed to living in obedience to him, because of the love they have for him, a place where loving your neighbor as yourself is normal behavior.

When considering whether the New Testament account of Jesus is reliable there is no more important claim to consider than the claim that Jesus rose from the dead. There is little doubt that he was crucified, since that fact is confirmed by secular accounts, but did he rise from the dead? The New Testament makes it clear that the disciples were devastated after the crucifixion. They believed that Jesus was bringing in a new kingdom that would free the Jewish people from Roman rule, so we cannot doubt that the sight of him hanging, apparently defeated, on a Roman cross would be enough to convince them that they must have got the wrong idea. According to Luke two of the disciples set off to walk from Jerusalem, where the crucifixion had taken place, to a nearby village. It was getting late so the light was probably failing when Jesus joined them and engaged them in conversation, so it is not surprising that they did not recognize him, especially when they had seen his dead body. Even if we suspend our judgment on who really walked with them, their conversation surely rings true. They tell this stranger about Jesus, whom they described as a prophet who was powerful in deeds and words and that they had trusted that he was the one who had come to set the Jews free from Rome, but they were obviously in despair as they said "it's getting on for three days since all this happened."[24] We get the same idea that it was the end of an era from John, who tells us that Peter and those of the other disciples, who had been fishermen, went back to their boats and started fishing again.[25] This is not at all difficult to believe, because they had followed Jesus expecting great things but now he was dead so they had better get back to the real world. It is the next step that needs careful consideration. This dispirited group of men came together with renewed vision to go out and preach the good news that Jesus had taught them. What would persuade these men to go out and invite the same painful death as their teacher if they believed he had misled them and ended his life in humiliation and defeat? We are forced to consider the claims they made, that Jesus had appeared to them after resurrection and convinced them that he was very much alive.

We face a similar situation when we consider the position of his half brothers, who are first introduced to us as unbelievers.[26] Jesus had left home and had started to proclaim his message but John tells us that his brothers did not believe him. It is not difficult to accept that the men who had grown up with Jesus found it hard to recognize that he was divine, indeed it is difficult to imagine what would change their minds, but something did. James, one of the half brothers of Jesus, became one of the church leaders and according to the Jewish historian Josephus was stoned to death in AD62. So what changed his mind? Paul gives us a list of the people to whom the risen Lord Jesus appeared and included in the list is Jesus' brother James.[27] James became known as James the Just because of the quality of his life and he was in a good position to know the quality of Jesus' life. James had seen the miracles of Jesus, he presumably knew the message Jesus preached and he must have regarded him as a good-living man, but was still not convinced that Jesus was the Savior that the Jews were waiting for. By AD 50, at the council of Jerusalem, James was a leader of the church in Jerusalem, prepared to die for his faith. The only explanation for his conversion and martyrdom was that he was visited by his half brother whom he knew to be dead and buried. Even after this experience James must also have recalled that the private life of Jesus, that he knew intimately, was consistent with who Jesus claimed to be. Only his memory of Jesus' consistently good life, together with a visit by Jesus after his resurrection, explains the change in James from unbeliever to one who would die for his belief in Jesus his Savior.

Finally we must consider the case of Paul the apostle, who by his own admission set out to destroy the church.[28] Paul was a devout Jew who found the teachings of Jesus offensive and according to Luke he stood and watched, with approval, the stoning to death of Stephen, one of the early Christians.[29] He then obtained permission from the Jewish authorities to pursue Jewish Christians throughout the Roman empire and bring them back to Jerusalem for punishment. Paul's case deserves special attention because as a prominent anti-Christian Jew in Jerusalem where Jesus was crucified and buried, he had access to the Temple authorities and any evidence that Jesus had not risen from the dead would be available to him. If, for example, they knew where the body of Jesus was buried, Paul would have known that the supposed resurrection was a sham. But when Paul set out on his mission to destroy the church he was confronted by the risen Lord Jesus and according to his own record this was the turning point for him.[30]

Jesus died after only three years of proclaiming his message, leaving only a small number of active followers who were so disheartened after his death that they returned to their former occupations, but after his resurrection they were galvanized into action. They claimed that Jesus had healed vast numbers of people and been raised from the dead. They made these claims in Jerusalem where the facts were well known and thousands of people were converted there. If there had been any doubt about either of their claims the disciples would have had no credibility and the message would have had little impact, but in fact this message spread quickly throughout the Roman Empire. Jesus has influenced more lives for good than any other person in history. His demand that his followers should love and offer help to people who hate them[31] is in contrast to the "eye for an eye" messages from other religious groups and "don't get mad get even" message in common usage today. Many years of persecution from the days of the Roman Empire through to today's communist and Islamic states have failed to extinguish the only message offering the certainty of eternal salvation.

Chapter 4

Faith and Science

At the start of the 19th century the belief in God was almost universal. Atheists had an uphill struggle to convince people that all the evidence of design that they saw around them was not due to the design of an active creator. Scientists such as Newton believed that they were involved in discovering the laws that God had used to control his creation and most people would have agreed with them. There were of course some dissenting voices; after all the Psalmist said "the fool has said in his heart there is no God"[1,2] and presumably he had knowledge of such people even 3000 years ago. Several atheist philosophers in the 18th and 19th centuries argued that the apparent design in the world around did not provide sufficient proof that there was a designer, but such arguments did not sway the majority of people.

In 1859 Darwin produced his classic book "The Origin of Species" and this had a great effect on popular opinion. It is worth noting that Darwin had his book published after a long period of deliberation because he realized that his theory might cause loss of faith in the Christian community and distress to his devout wife. He published in a hurry when he heard that Alfred Russell Wallace had developed the same idea and was also writing a book on the subject. Darwin, however, still had some belief in God and he concluded his final edition of the book with the thought that the evolutionary flow of life was initiated by "its several powers having been originally breathed by the creator in a few life forms or into one"[3] This gives the impression that Darwin came to his conclusions from his observations but still saw them as a result of the creative hand of God.

As he suspected however this was not the viewpoint of the intellectual atheists of the time, who saw Darwin's theory as a way of viewing the design of the world as a lucky accident giving them the intellectual support for their atheistic beliefs.

Evolution is discussed in a later chapter so in this chapter we will consider whether the Bible is reasonable when it says "the heavens declare the glory of God; the skies proclaim the work of his hands"[4] or are atheists correct when they say that we are just benefiting from the results of probability? Just how lucky would we have to be to be surrounded by a universe of such incredible order?

Until the 1920s the majority of scientists believed that the universe was in a state where the heavenly bodies were, and always had been, in stable positions relative to each other, that suited atheists just fine. It did away with the need to explain creation or even consider God. When it was established that the Universe was expanding it clearly suggested a starting point when time and space were created. Mathematical theory allowed for the possibility that the universe is expanding at an ever decreasing rate, being slowed down by gravitational attraction. When the heavenly bodies slowed sufficiently and gravitational attraction became dominant, all matter in the universe would return to a single point from which it could expand again. This view of an eternally oscillating universe was seized on by atheists because it postulates a universe without a creation. Further examination of the problem, however, showed that each successive cycle would result in a higher ratio of photons to nuclear particles.[5] The universe that would result from the infinite number of cycles that atheists require to eliminate a beginning would be a universe with no solid matter, that clearly is not what exists. Recent observations have shown that the universe is expanding at an ever increasing rate which is incompatible with the oscillating universe theory.

Scientists have used the current observations of the universe and the accepted principles of science to derive a standard model of the early universe. This is popularly known as the "big bang theory" that describes the creation of time and space. This theory, that was developed as a result of Einstein's General Theory of Relativity together with the observation that the universe was expanding, came under continual attack until late in the 20th century, because it lends itself to an explanation involving a divine creator. Despite these objections the big bang theory is generally accepted today. We now need to look at a few important facts so that we can examine the significance of the big bang theory.

Einstein's famous equation $E=mc^2$ describes the fact that matter can be turned into energy. In a nuclear reactor energy is obtained as a result of the fission process. In the reactor the nucleus of a heavy fissionable material is made unstable and splits into two lighter atoms. The mass of the fission products is less than that of the fissionable material and the reduction in mass results in an output of energy in accordance with Einstein's equation. This idea of mass turning into energy is now well known, but it is also possible to turn energy into matter. When this is done in the laboratory the result is one particle of antimatter for each particle of matter, but the two particles quickly recombine, reverting to radiation.

We must next consider light. What we call light is one part of the spectrum of electromagnetic radiation that includes many phenomena that we often think of as totally separate. These include infra red radiation that is emitted by our warm bodies and many supermarkets use this to open their doors as we approach them. It also includes radio frequency radiation that carries radio and television signals from the transmitter to our homes and radar that is used to guide aircraft safely to the airport runway, even when visibility is poor. All these different forms of radiation can be thought of as a stream of packets of energy called photons. The photons carry frequency information with them and this frequency defines the class of radiation, light, ultra violet etc. The amount of energy carried by each photon is proportional to its frequency.

The "big bang" is envisaged as an explosion that occurred throughout the newly created space. The resulting very high temperature was too great for any atoms or molecules to hold together, so all that existed consisted of elementary particles and photons. It is believed that this early creation of particles from energy must have included almost equal quantities of matter and antimatter. Had the number of particles of matter been equal to the number of particles of antimatter which is always seen in physics laboratories when matter is created from energy, the result would have been the complete annihilation of matter leaving a universe with no material content. The first bit of remarkable luck or careful design is that there was a surplus of matter over antimatter, since everything we see around us is made from that surplus.

The initial rate of expansion of the universe was much greater than it is today and it had to oppose the force of gravity that was working to pull the creation back together. The balance between the repulsive force of the big bang and the attractive force of gravity had to be delicately balanced for the result to be the universe we now see. Had the force of the big bang been weaker the cosmos would soon have collapsed in a big crunch. If the big bang had been stronger the cosmic material would have dispersed so rapidly that galaxies would have been unable to form. Professor Davies tells us that if the initial explosion had differed in strength by one part in 10^{60} the universe we now perceive would not exist.[6]

It is thought that after about 3 minutes the temperature had cooled sufficiently for the nuclei of deuterium (one proton and one neutron) and helium (two protons and two neutrons) to have formed and this matter continued to cool whilst expanding at great speed. Further cooling allowed the atoms of hydrogen and helium to form after a few hundred thousand years.[7] In order for the heavy elements, such as iron to be formed it was necessary for these light gases to be pulled together by gravity into stars in which nuclear fusion takes place. It is believed that a first generation of these stars produced all the stable elements so that when the earth was formed, its structure would include iron, tin and copper in large quantities. Carbon would also be available to form the long chain molecules that make up our bodies.

We will now briefly consider entropy and the second law of thermodynamics. Entropy is defined by the Encyclopedia Britannica as a measure of a system's energy that is unavailable for work. The second law of thermodynamics says that all thermodynamic systems can move in one direction only and the opposite direction that would return the system to its original state is impossible (without external effort) because no systems whether they are chemical, biological or mechanical are 100% efficient. This can also be stated as work always produces an increase in entropy. Let us consider this for a moment. There are two electricity generating plants in Wales that derive their power from the potential energy stored in a lake on top of a mountain. The water passes down a shaft from the top of the mountain to the bottom passing through an electricity generator. The power plants can produce up to 1800 Megawatts of power within 10 seconds of being switched on, that means they can meet sudden high energy demands with a response time far faster than coal or oil driven power stations. As the upper lake is emptied into the lake below the entropy of the system is increasing because entropy is a measure of the energy in the system that is no longer available to do work. The potential energy that the water had at the top of the mountain has partially been converted into kinetic energy, moving the rotor of the generator, that has converted the energy into electrical power. When the water leaves the shaft it is collected in a lower lake, that has less potential energy than the upper lake, so the overall system has less energy available to do work and therefore has a higher entropy. When the main electrical power stations are producing surplus electricity, usually in the early hours of the morning, the generator blades in the shaft between the lakes use this surplus electricity to turn in the reverse direction, pumping the water back up into the higher lake ready for the next peak demand. The electrical energy required to pump the water up is always higher than the energy generated when the lake emptied. This is because of losses in the system, such as heat generated in the electrical cables and the result is an increase in net entropy. All activities in the universe result in a net increase in entropy.

The majority of the energy available to us comes from the sun. This is because the sun is at a higher temperature than the earth and therefore the sun supplies the earth with a steady supply of high energy photons. This energy is converted by plants into food that animals can digest and that we can use to enable us to live and do work. We also use trees and coal, whose creation was only possible due to the existence of the sun, to produce heat to drive machines and do work for us. The sun will eventually run out of hydrogen and be unable to produce any more heat and the same will happen to all the other suns. Scientists predict that the universe will eventually reach a state where the universe is all at an even temperature, when it will have no ability to support life or any useful work, a condition of the universe that has been described as "heat death." The big bang produced a universe with very low entropy and Professor Roger Penrose has examined the possible conditions of the initial universe and came to the conclusion that it would have been much more likely that the universe be formed in a high entropy state. If that had been the case there would have existed a very different universe, unable to support life. He concludes that the probability that the low entropy universe, that we inhabit, to have come about by chance is almost zero. He imagines an extremely large volume of space in which every point represents a different possible starting condition for the universe and states that "In order to produce a universe resembling the one in which we live, the creator would have to aim for an absurdly tiny volume of the phase space of possible universes."[8] If the universe arose by pure chance, we only exist because the creation chose several paths of almost zero probability.

Now let us look at the properties of some of the materials we depend on, that atheists believe to have come about as a result of pure chance. Many substances make a unique contribution to our ability to function normally and we will now examine a few of these.

All the material things around us are made from only 92 naturally occurring elements and a large proportion of these have unique properties without which life as we know it would be impossible. We can consider these elements to be made up of three building blocks: protons and neutrons, that combine to form the nucleus of the atom, and electrons that surround the nucleus (ignoring the fact that these elementary particles can be split into still smaller quarks). The protons have a positive electric charge and the electrons have a negative electric charge. The atom of any element contains the same number of protons as electrons making it electrically neutral. The electrons can only exist in a number of discrete states, each with a defined energy level and the number of electrons that surround the nucleus give each of the elements their distinctive chemical properties. If the electrons were not limited to these discrete energy levels they would collapse into the nucleus and none of the chemical bonding on which life depends could take place.

The universe and all its components are held in their state of relative motion by the action of various forces. At present four basic forces are known although it is the goal of many physicists to show that at very high temperature they combine into one universal force.[9] The force of gravity is a force of attraction between two separate objects with mass. It is a relatively weak force but as it is proportional to the mass of the objects it can have a great effect when large masses like the earth or the sun are involved. Gravity keeps our feet on the ground and the earth revolving around the sun and is still active even at very large separations, but it does decrease with the square of the distance of separation. Doubling the distance between two masses results in reducing the attractive force to a quarter of its former value. At the initial creation all the mass of the universe was concentrated in a very small volume so the force of attraction holding it together would have been enormous, but an even larger creative force was required to cause it to disperse.

The second basic force is the electromagnetic force. This causes attraction between a positive and a negative charge, but repulsion between particles with like charges. Within the atom the attraction between the positively charged protons in the nucleus and the negatively charged electrons around it keep the electrons from escaping from the atom, and provides the force to keep the electrons orbiting around the nucleus. Without this force none of the elements could be formed and life would be impossible. This force is effective over large distances and, like gravity, decreases with increasing separation.

The remaining two basic forces are the strong and weak nuclear forces that act at such small distances that they only take effect within the atomic structure. The strong force keeps the nucleus together, working against the electrostatic repulsion of the positively charged protons. Without the strong force electrostatic repulsion of the protons would scatter the nuclear particles, preventing the formation of the elements and compounds on which life depends. A rather small change in the relative balance between the electrostatic repulsion of the protons and the attractive strong nuclear force would disrupt the balance between them and no stable elements would exist. The fact that the electron is so much lighter than the proton is also critical, because if its mass were a few times greater, gravitational attraction between electrons and protons would add to their electrostatic attraction. This would result in them combining to form neutrons. The result would be that hydrogen atoms, that are made up of one proton and one electron would not exist. The fusion of hydrogen atoms provides the power of the sun and is a vital element for living things. No other element could replace hydrogen as an energy source, so the balance of forces and masses that enable it to exist is the result of good design or immense good fortune.

The relative weakness of the force of gravity has produced other beneficial results. Gravity holds the mass of the sun together and if its attractive power were reduced the sun would never have formed. If gravitational attraction were increased significantly however the sun's mass would bind more closely and the rate of nuclear reactions would increase. The sun would then have a bright life but a short one and the long period of constant, steady heat and light that the sun has provided would be impossible. We must also note that it is important that the strong nuclear force has no effect on the electrons because that would disrupt the exact balance between the positive charge on the protons and the negative charge on the electrons.

The fourth force is the weak force, that like the strong nuclear force only acts within the nucleus, and is responsible for the fission, or breaking up, of heavy radioactive materials into lighter elements. Because of its weak value relative to the strong force, radioactive elements such as the isotopes of Uranium decay over very long periods of time so that despite the age of the earth there are still useful quantities in the earth's surface to provide energy for us to use in nuclear reactors. The balance between the four basic forces and the masses of the nuclear particles is absolutely critical. If the laws that govern these forces were pure chance, the probability of ending up with exactly the correct values to make the elements stable and life possible, from an infinity of possibilities, would be extremely small.[10]

We are now going to look at a number substances with unique physical properties so that we can see how they make life as we know it possible. It is not my intention to give an exhaustive coverage of the properties of these substances that make them essential to life, but to lead the reader to the conclusion that we are either beneficiaries of the work of a careful designer or of amazing good fortune. Greater detail can be found in the references. [11,12]

Water

Water is essential to life as we know it and it covers two thirds of the earth's surface, so we have a plentiful supply. If there is any water on other planets in our solar system it is in relatively small amounts. The water in the oceans contains too much salt for humans to drink except in small quantities, but it supports a great variety of fish and continuous evaporation of pure water from the oceans forms clouds. These clouds can drift thousands of miles to provide fresh water over much of the earth, so that there is plenty of pure, drinkable water for most people, especially if they learn to conserve it while ensuring that they don't waste or pollute it.

When a liquid is frozen it turns into a solid and we would intuitively think that the solid would be more dense than the liquid. The solid state of almost all substances is more dense than its liquid state but water has its maximum density at 3.94 degrees centigrade at normal atmospheric pressure, therefore ice is less dense than water. A frozen lake usually supports the ice at the surface with water whose density increases with increasing depth, when the status of the lake is said to be stable. Another important fact is that the thermal conductivity of ice is only a quarter of that of water. This means that when a lake freezes an ice layer forms on top and acts as a blanket to the water below. This allows the fish and plant life in the lake to live. If ice were more dense than water, lakes and rivers would freeze from the bottom and destroy the fish and much of the plant life. In parts of the earth with long winters many lakes, especially shallow ones, would freeze completely and the ice on the bottom of these lakes would never melt, making it difficult for them to support any life.

The specific heat of a liquid is the amount of heat required to raise the temperature of a unit mass of that liquid by one degree. The specific heat of water is higher than that of most other liquids and this means that it can absorb large amounts of heat in the tropics whilst increasing in temperature by a modest amount. This keeps the coastal areas in the tropics at a relatively low temperature during the summer. The ocean currents take this warm water to cold areas of the earth where the winters by the coasts are far less severe because of the heat in the oceans.

A further property of water that is of utmost importance to warm blooded humans is its latent heat of evaporation that has a greater value than for any other liquid, at normal ambient temperatures. When a liquid changes into a gas it requires a quantity of heat, that does not raise its temperature but is used to perform the change of state. The metabolism of living creatures like all working engines produces heat as a by product and this must be efficiently removed from the body. Heat could be removed from the body in three ways: radiation, conduction or convection. The temperature of our bodies would need to be much higher for radiation to be an efficient means of heat removal. Air is not a good thermal conductor (if it were we could not approach a hot object) so removing sufficient heat by conduction involves covering the body with a cold substance such as ice or water. This is hardly convenient when engaged in strenuous activity so we depend on perspiration to keep our bodies cool. The perspiration is then turned into vapor by our bodies' excess heat and removed by convection. The fact that the control system in our bodies keeps our temperature constant to within a fraction of a degree, under all normal circumstances, is only possible because of the high value of the latent heat of evaporation of water. To be clear, life would be possible if this value were considerably lower but we would be very limited in our ability to work hard for an extensive period of time. An atheist must believe that our luck is amazing!

The viscosity of a substance is a measure of its resistance to having its shape changed. If you pour water on a flat surface it quickly runs all over it because its viscosity is low. Honey poured onto the same surface would slowly creep across it because the viscosity of honey is high. Water has a viscosity that is lower than almost all other liquids and Michael Denton[13] argues that its value could not be much different for life to exist as we know it. In humans the tissues are provided with essential nutrients by the blood stream. Blood flows through tiny capillaries that permeate the body and provide the cells with oxygen and glucose whilst removing waste products. The walls of these capillaries have to be very thin because transfer to and from the cells takes place by diffusion through the cell wall, so the pressure of the blood cannot be too high or the capillaries would rupture. The diameter of the tube through which a liquid flows determines the resistance to flow, the narrower the tube the greater the resistance. It follows that the only way to get blood through the narrow capillaries at a pressure that will not rupture their thin walls is for its viscosity to be very low, which it is, as blood plasma is more than 90% water. We may be tempted to think that any low value of viscosity will do, but as Denton points out cells require some rigidity so that they have some resistance to deformation and the viscosity of water is high enough to give this degree of stability. As we would expect, the flow of water through a pipe is proportional to the pressure difference along the length of the pipe, at moderate rates of flow. To double the flow you have to double the pressure. We have seen it is important for the blood to get to the cells it sustains with as little pressure as possible, so that the very thin capillary walls do not rupture. This is aided by a decline in the viscosity of water when small particles are added to it. Blood has a viscous behavior similar to water with the addition of blood cells, that act like small particles, resulting in approximately triple the blood flow when the pressure is doubled. This apparently trivial property is in fact vital because when we undertake a strenuous activity such as running, the blood supply to the muscles may need to increase by twenty times. The heart can achieve this increase in flow with a relatively small increase in pressure only because of the non linear change of viscosity due to the blood cells. Once again, if blood did not have this property life would be possible but much more difficult.

Carbon

It is not an exaggeration to say that all known life is carbon based, depending as it does on the unique properties of this element. Compounds are formed by combining different elements and more than a million compounds of carbon are known.

We have mentioned that elements are made up of a nucleus, where most of the mass resides, and a surrounding cloud of electrons. Lord Rutherford performed his famous scattering experiment at Manchester University, that proved that the nucleus occupies a very small volume of any material. The greatest volume of any solid consists of space in which the electrons are held by electrostatic attraction to the protons in the nucleus. The number of protons in the nucleus is called the atomic number and for the atom to be neutral the number of electrons must equal the number of protons. The carbon atom has six electrons, four of which are called valency electrons, because they are available to combine with valency electrons in other atoms to form covalent bonds. Covalent bonds are formed when an atom shares its valency electrons with those of other atoms so that the combination of atoms forms a molecule with lower energy than that possessed by the free atoms. As an example, hydrogen has only one valency electron so the carbon atom can share its four valency electrons with four hydrogen atoms to form methane gas CH_4. Now other elements can form covalent bonds but the carbon atom is able to join together with other carbon atoms to form long, stable chains or rings to which can be added a wide variety of other atoms. Carbon combines with hydrogen, oxygen and nitrogen to form amino acids that are the building blocks of proteins. Proteins are fundamental to the structure of DNA on which all life depends. Without carbon and its unique properties that enable the long instruction chains needed to specify the functions of our cells, life as complex as ours would be inconceivable. All the vital structures of living organisms depend on the unique properties of carbon. Spectral analysis of the light from around the universe shows that the only elements are the ones we know on earth and the only element other than carbon to form long chains is silicon. But the carbon to carbon bond is much stronger than the silicon to silicon bond and as Brown[14] says silicon–silicon bonds are open to attack by water that adds to their instability. So it is accepted that no known substance could take the place of carbon in basic life chemistry and no silicon based life has been discovered on earth.

Oxygen

We live in an atmosphere containing about 21% oxygen, a level that is almost constant. All animals require a way of producing energy and this requires a chemical process that is efficient and produces waste products that are not harmful. When oxygen combines with other elements it releases more energy than that released by any other element except fluorine. In oxidizing hydrogen and carbon the body utilizes two reactions that produce very large amounts of energy, in fact the oxidation of hydrogen produces far more energy than the oxidation of any other element. The basic energy producing reaction within the cell results in safe byproducts as shown and amazingly plants are able to use the energy of sunlight to reverse the process.

Animal Respiration >>>>

Glucose + oxygen = water + carbon dioxide + Energy

$$C_6H_{12}O_6 + 6O_2 = 6CO_2 + 6H_2O \ (+ \ Energy)$$

<<<< Plant Photosynthesis (Sunlight)

    This process of oxidizing hydrocarbons to produce energy with the oxygen molecules available in the atmosphere is only possible because of the catalytic action of a number of enzymes produced by the cell, and of course the cell needs energy to produce the enzymes! The cell also needs energy to enable it to do work such as the transport of waste products, muscle contraction, the electrical work of transmitting nerve impulses and the chemical work of forming the bonds of the molecules that are synthesized in the cell. Much of the energy is stored in high energy compounds such as ATP (adenosine triphosphate) that provide the energy at the precise place where it is required. The processes required use the unique properties of many materials that are described further in the references, but we will mention the properties of Cytochrome c oxidase that is regarded by one prominent biochemist as the enzyme most vital to life. This substance combines the properties of iron and copper to introduce oxygen into the energy production process of the cell. This not only highlights the unique value of oxygen to life but introduces two further elements whose properties are vital to life.[15,16]

We might ask if a 21% concentration of oxygen in the atmosphere is the result of a careful plan or will any value suffice. We are well aware that lower values would make life more difficult. Just climbing to the top of a high mountain requires climbers to take a supply of oxygen with them, but perhaps any higher percentage will do just fine. It turns out that is not the case. The air around us contains mainly oxygen molecules that are quite stable at normal atmospheric temperatures and pressures but their reactivity increases greatly above 50 degrees centigrade. We know from experience how difficult it can be to light a fire but how fierce it can be once it gets hot. Denton tells us that the probability of forest fires being started by lightning increases by up to 70% for every 1 per cent increase in atmospheric oxygen.[17] If the concentration ever rose above 25% a great deal of our land vegetation would be destroyed in the resulting fires. If it is chance that controls the level of oxygen in the atmosphere the fact that it is fixed at a value within a fairly narrow optimum range is very fortunate indeed.

The solubility of oxygen in water is important to fish, which extract oxygen from the sea, but it is also important to mankind because the oxygen in the lungs has to pass through a thin aqueous layer to reach the red blood cells and convert hemoglobin into oxyhemoglobin. The oxygen must pass through a further aqueous layer when it reaches the tissues, where the oxygen is removed and replaced with carbon dioxide, a waste product of the respiration process. The blood then carries the carbon dioxide to the lungs that excrete it into the air. Whilst the oxygen atom is extremely reactive, most of the oxygen in the atmosphere at normal altitudes consists of O_2 molecules that are quite inert below 50 degrees centigrade. The body uses a number of specialized enzymes that harness the properties of transition metal atoms such as iron and copper to make oxygen highly reactive and available where required. The waste product carbon dioxide slowly hydrates into carbonic acid, a weak acid, that dissociates into hydrogen ions and bicarbonate. Body fluids are slightly basic but the red blood cells use the enzyme carbonic anhydrase to control the rate of formation of carbonic acid and thus control the acidity of the body. If carbonic acid was a strong acid or produced quickly it could not be used to control body acidity. We must conclude that the unique chemical and physical properties of carbon dioxide and oxygen make them essential to life.

In this brief account we have only touched the surface of the many materials whose unique properties make life possible.

Sunlight

The spectrum of electromagnetic radiation ranges from cosmic rays with a frequency of around 10^{22} Hz to low frequency radio waves oscillating at frequencies as low as 3 Hz (ELF band). The majority of the radiation from the sun is restricted to a narrow band of frequencies from 1.4×10^{16} Hz to 2×10^{14} Hz, that is a tiny fraction of the possible bandwidth. This limited band of radiation from the sun includes all the frequencies visible to humans with the addition of some infrared and ultraviolet radiation.

The fact that the sensitivity of the human eye is entirely within the range of sunlight may indicate God's design to the Christian but the evolutionist will say natural selection would produce this result. But human life on earth depends on the action of photosynthesis by which plants turn the energy of sunlight into energy they can use to grow. The Encyclopedia Britannica states that "If photosynthesis ceased there would soon be little food or organic matter on earth and in time earth's atmosphere would become nearly devoid of oxygen:"[18] In other words photosynthesis is both vital to life on the surface of earth and unique in its function. Photosynthesis is accomplished by a complex series of reactions that are initiated by the action of sunlight on the chlorophyll in cells of green plants or in one-celled organisms. The radiation that initiates photosynthesis has a mean frequency of about 5.25×10^{14} Hz, that is right in the visible range: radiation at higher frequencies can destroy the plant cells, whilst radiation at lower frequencies cannot trigger the chemical reaction. The fact that the tiny spectrum of light emitted from the sun includes the exact value required by plants to grow and thereby sustain almost all life on the planet is another phenomenon whose probability of occurring by chance is very low. There is no way that the frequency required to activate photosynthesis could have been aligned with the radiation from the sun by a 'selfish gene' or the 'force of evolution'. The system was designed that way or we were extraordinarily lucky.

Atheist evolutionists congratulate themselves because they have invented a possible path for the evolution of the eye which, although speculation, they believe eliminates the need to consider a designer. But the eye is a water based organ depending on the ability of water to pass light through it. Water is transparent to visible light but becomes opaque to radiation just above and just below the visible spectrum. A water based eye is only feasible for radiation in the frequency range of the Sun's emissions. The eye may or may not have evolved without external intervention but the physical properties of water which make the eye possible appear to have been carefully tailored, and they owe nothing to evolution.

The Atmosphere

The beneficial properties of sunlight would be of little use to us if it was unable to penetrate the atmosphere. Denton tells us that the great majority of all atoms are completely opaque to visible light and radiation in the near infrared region.[19] The earth's atmosphere however allows 80% of the sun's radiation in the visible and near infrared region to reach the earth's surface whilst filtering out almost all other radiation that could be harmful to life. The range of frequencies that reach the earth's surface after the atmosphere has filtered out much of the incident ultraviolet radiation is very small indeed, but this is one of only two frequency ranges of the electromagnetic spectrum where radiation does not damage life. The other safe radiation is long radio waves that we use for communication.[20] We have seen how important the transparency of the atmosphere is to visible light both for our vision and for photosynthesis, but why should transparency to near infra red be important? Penrose tells us that the earth's surface temperature remains fairly constant because the energy falling on the earth as visible light is balanced by an equal amount of infrared energy radiated by earth into space.[21] This infrared energy must be able to get through the atmosphere or the earth's temperature would rise continuously.

The historical argument of the atheist was that the fact that we exist doesn't prove the existence of a creator and even the singular properties of nature that make life possible are no proof because if they were different we simply would never have existed. This argument is much weaker now we know that there was a time when the universe was created, anathema to the atheist who requires eternal continuity. We also know three vital facts about the creation. Firstly, that the universe was created in a low entropy state, secondly, that the creation resulted in an excess of matter over antimatter and thirdly, that the force of the initial expansion was finely balanced for creation of the universe. All three of these outcomes had extremely low probabilities. The existence of stable elements is only possible because of the fine balance between the masses of the components of the atom and the forces between them. In addition the unique properties of many elements and compounds are required to make life possible and they give very strong indications of being designed for their purpose. It is also true that we could have existed under very inferior conditions to those in which we find ourselves. We have been provided with an abundance of natural resources, coal, oil, gas, iron, copper, lead, tin, fertile land, fresh water over much of the earth and much more. The low electrical resistance of copper and the magnetic properties of iron, that are both abundant, have transformed modern life, enabling the development of distributed electrical power and motor driven appliances. The physical properties of silicon have made it possible for millions of people to have computing power in their homes beyond the dreams of the Ferranti engineers who shipped the first commercial computer from Manchester in 1951. We could certainly survive without the quantities of these natural resources, but their provision on such a vast scale suggests a caring provider.

In his classic work on natural Theology, William Paley imagined himself walking across a heath and finding two items there: a stone and a watch. Paley suggested that whilst the stone tells him little about whether its creation was by design or accident, the watch is clearly the result of intelligent design and indeed implies a watchmaker. He then went on to describe various parts of the human body that, he claimed pointed to a designer as clearly as the watch demanded the existence of a watchmaker. Atheist evolutionists after Darwin ascribed this design to the "force of evolution" but we can see that the physical world presents us with a picture of precision far greater than any watchmaker achieved.

The evangelical atheist Dawkins insists that we should choose what we believe on the basis of probability.[22] The probability is negligibly small that all the listed unlikely events that resulted in the creation of the earth could have occurred by blind chance:

1) The precision of the initial "big bang" that overcame the initial force of attraction but that resulted in a universe that is expanding slowly enough for galaxies to form.
2) The creation of a universe with a low entropy.
3) A creation that resulted in an excess of matter over antimatter.
4) The precise structure of the atom with its balance of forces and its accurate quantum energy levels for electrons resulting in 92 stable, natural elements.
5) The availability of 92 elements, many of which are used in the human body. Several of these elements have unique properties that make life as we know it possible.
6) The presence on earth of large quantities of materials such as oil, iron, sulphur, copper, coal, salt, calcium phosphate (for fertiliser) etc., etc. The list of materials that are in abundant supply and make modern life possible is very long.
7) The abundance of sunlight that reaches the earth. Sunlight includes only a very small part of the possible range of radiation frequencies, but includes the frequency range required for photosynthesis: a process essential to life.

8) The properties of the atmosphere that lets radiation, that is necessary for life, penetrate through it whilst filtering out most of the dangerous radiation.

The precision we find in creation cannot be the result of a "force of evolution" and we must decide whether it is due to careful design or the result a series of extremely improbable events. I contend that it points to a creator who has watched over the details of his creation with great care.

We make many decisions on the basis of probability, not absolute certainty. We board a plane knowing that there is a real possibility that it will crash and we will be killed, but that the probability is small. If one in ten aircraft crashed there would be few people ready to fly. If you were to win the lottery you could say that you were lucky, but in all fairness someone has to win at reasonable intervals or no one would play. If you won again the next month people would be surprised but think it was possible. If you won month after month the authorities would certainly take an interest in your affairs because they would be sure that you had found a way to cheat the system. The facts are that if you won the lottery on every occasion from your eighteenth birthday until you were 90 you would not have beaten the odds by nearly so much as we have by having so many things in creation work together to make our lives possible, if they are the result of blind chance. When the writers in the enlightenment wrote about the universe as we see it being the result of chance they had no concept of the odds against that being the case, but their writings are used in arguments against the existence of God to this day. To say that anything that could happen will happen has no basis in fact. We have no evidence to say that there are any other stable elements than the ones we have detected throughout the universe or any life forms that are based on any other chemistry than that which we have on earth. The other suggestion by atheists that there exists an infinity of universes with every possible variation of composition has no basis in observed fact, and is beyond the realm of experimental science.

I may not have absolutely proved that the universe has been created by a brilliant designer who had intelligent life on earth as one of his goals, but surely an unbiassed person would have to conclude that this was the most likely possibility by far.

As I complete this chapter, the scientific world is struggling to assimilate the results of a recent experiment at CERN that appeared to show it is possible for a neutrino to travel at speeds greater than the speed of light. The assumption that the speed of light is the highest speed that can be achieved is fundamental to the theoretical work of Einstein and to his conclusions about relativity. It must be said that many previous experiments have supported Einstein's work and other measurements of the speeds of neutrinos indicated that they did not exceed the speed of light. If the speed of light has been exceeded it will result in the need for a fundamental review of modern physics. Regardless of the final outcome of this research, it serves to remind us that today's science will be regarded as primitive by the science community of 2200AD. With that in mind, it is surprising that some atheists imagine that they can dispute vehemently the existence of God on the basis of today's imperfect knowledge.

Chapter 5

The Problem of Evolution

Shortly after I left University I joined a church with two members who had strong views on evolution. One was a Biology teacher at a local University, who was an evolutionist. The second was a distinguished surgeon who did not accept evolution. This diversity of viewpoints was quite acceptable in the church and neither individual had any problem worshipping together while agreeing on the fundamental teachings in the Bible. I held both these fellow worshippers in high regard and recognized that both of them knew more about evolution than I did, so I kept an open mind on the subject until I had time to study the facts. This diversity of views is still found in the church and in publications by Christians, but atheists continually try to use this theory as a weapon against the church, so it is a subject that we must consider. It is important to recognize that atheists approach nature with the fundamental hypothesis that there is no God, a hypothesis that they are unable to prove, but that forces them to explain everything in a natural way. The Christian has the freedom to accept or reject theories that are not proved, but is confronted with the situation where atheists have an incomplete theory for the creation of life on earth, based on the hypothesis that there is no God. They then claim that evolution is proved and on this basis some of them attempt to use evolution as proof that there is no God.

When Darwin published his Origin of the Species[1] he knew that it was far from a proof of his theory and he included discussions of the many problems that he could see with his ideas. The general belief today is that the main objection to Darwin came from church leaders and because their opposition was inadequate, atheism triumphed. In fact a great deal of opposition came from scientists who did not think that the case for evolution had been made, so let us look at what Darwin claimed and the scientific objections to his claim.

Darwin had observed the variations that had occurred in populations of animals, in isolated regions such as the Galapagos islands and in domestic animals that had been selectively bred to obtain desirable characteristics. Darwin also came under the influence of Thomas Robert Malthus who wrote an essay called the "Principle of Population" in which he suggested that, as the world's population was growing geometrically, it would soon be too large for the world's food supply, resulting in mass starvation. Such was the impact of this paper that the British Prime Minister, William Pitt, withdrew his support for a parliamentary bill to give aid to the poor, in case it encouraged them to have more children, thereby propelling the world into the imminent famine that Malthus erroneously predicted.[2] Darwin drew the lesson from Malthus that the animal kingdom was too large for the supply of food, resulting in continual conflict. This he believed would enable only the animals that were best equipped to live off the available food supply to survive, whilst animal species that were not so well adapted died off. Darwin believed that the cumulation of successful adaptations would, in time, lead to new species emerging. He had seen what he believed to be the results of this action, by observation of animals and plants on the Galapagos islands, where several species had adapted to local conditions in isolation from the mainland populations. For example the islands' finches exhibited variations of bill shape and size, enabling different varieties of finch to be more efficient hunters of their particular prey. This was one example of many where small variations of size or color made individuals with those characteristics more efficient feeders, or better able to avoid their predators. Such animals became dominant in isolated areas and in time became new species. Darwin believed that an extension of this process could, by a series of small random adaptations, lead from a simple, mono-cellular life form to a primate. The leap from a selection process between the birds with the most suitable beak for survival to the formation of a wing on a creature without one is obviously massive, but this is what Darwin proposed. Darwin did not perform scientific experiments to prove any part of his theory. Experimental evidence had to wait until the 1950s when Bernard Kettlewell, an Oxford zoologist, conducted a series of experiments in which he released a mixed group of dark and light moths at two different locations. He was able to show that, when released in an unpolluted forest the light colored moths survived in much larger numbers, but when released in polluted city woods, it was the darker moths that survived preferentially.[3] Today it is accepted that pink daisies can evolve into blue daisies and light moth populations can become dark moth populations in different surroundings, but even if the differences become so great that new species, that can no longer propagate with the parent population, are developed, they are still daisies and moths. This is called micro evolution and clearly can be explained by the natural variations within a species and the domination of the variety most suited to survive in a particular environment. Micro evolution is proved beyond doubt, it is the leap to macro evolution that Darwin made that is without proof to this day.

Before we get too far ahead we should deal with a popular misconception that formed no part of

Dawin's theory but appears to be implied from time to time when evolution is discussed. By this theory, postulated by Lamark, variations could be achieved by need and effort. So the giraffe's long neck was achieved by short necked ancestors stretching up to reach higher and higher foliage. This theory is completely discredited, therefore it is no part of any accepted theory that if you swing from tree branches all your life it will result in your progeny having longer arms. Evolutionists occasionally lapse into statements that are very close to Lamarkian however, such as a statement on the Internet that the Cambrian explosion, an historic period when great changes occurred in the animal kingdom in a relatively short period of time, may have been caused by the first creature to develop an eye. The suggestion was that once one creature had an eye its ability to survive was so enhanced that other creatures had to develop eyes also to survive. If evolution takes place through completely chance mutations the fact that one creature had an eye would have no effect on the time it took for other creatures to develop an eye. They would have to wait for a similar series of chance mutations to create an eye for them. Competing with a creature that could see would clearly be easier for some animals, those with acute hearing or with an ultrasonic sound detection system, like a bat, for example, but evolution would only provide sight for other animals by chance.

A second misconception that is widely encouraged by textbooks on evolution is that the similarity of external appearance indicates a close relationship. The shark and the dolphin are similar in appearance but one is a mammal and one is a fish and no close relationship can be drawn from this similarity.

The mechanism that Darwin proposed for macro evolution was that simple chance variations that were beneficial to a species would result in that variation becoming dominant in that region. If this region were isolated from the parent population the resulting variants could in time become a new species. This would mean that all apparent design was in fact the result of blind chance. It is clear that the individual changes that this system could generate would be very small and the number of gradual changes to evolve a bird from an amphibian would involve the creation of many thousands of intermediate animals, all of which would need to be at least as capable of survival as their forebears in order to meet Darwin's criteria. This led to a problem because the fossil record known to Darwin revealed distinct groupings of animals and plants, that had been classified over many years with no known links between these groups. Darwin recognized the problem and considered that it was due to the very small number of fossils that had been examined at that time and he expected that in time thousands of missing links would be uncovered. Today many lifetimes of work have gone into uncovering hundreds of thousands of fossils all over the world and there are no uncontested missing links that bridge the distinct animal groups. There are a small number of fossils that have some of the characteristics of two major animal classes, such as the archaeopteryx that has bird-like wings but a jaw and teeth like an amphibian, however there is little doubt that it was a complete creature. Its wings were completely formed just like a bird's and there is no proof that it was anything other than one of a number of unusual creatures. If he were alive today Darwin would still be unable to use the argument that the fossil record unambiguously supports his gradual evolution theory because it doesn't, but that does not stop popular science suggesting that it does.

Prior to Darwin, biologists had a typological model of the organic world in which animals were divided into different types that were completely distinct from one another. Contemporary biologists such as Cuvier and Agassiz objected to evolution on the grounds of the distinctive nature of the animal types and the lack of intermediates. They believed that each organism belonged in a grouping, such as mammals or birds, that could be described by features that applied equally to all members of that group. So birds are described as warm blooded vertebrates with feathers and a four chambered heart who lay eggs with a calcareous shell and who have a unique respiratory system. Mammals are vertebrate animals whose young are nourished from special secreting glands. They grow hair and have a lower jaw hinged directly to the skull. A chain of three tiny bones transmits sound waves across the middle ear. They also have a muscular diaphragm that separates the heart and the lungs from the abdominal cavity. A further characteristic of mammals is that they have red blood cells without a nucleus unlike all other vertebrates.

The basic types of animals are called phyla and they can be subdivided into class, order, family, genus and finally species. So for an example from the phylum "Chordata" we can select the class of "mammal," the order of "carnivora," the family of "felidae," and the genus of "panthera."[4] This could be further subdivided into species, two examples of which are the lion and tiger. It should be noted that the lion and tiger are close relatives and they can be used in captivity to produce a crossbreed called a tigon (or liger), but this, like the ass, is sterile. It is therefore clear that a chance change in a single member of any species that resulted in an individual separated from its parent population by as large a difference as that existing between a lion and a tiger would not result in any change to the species, since it could not propagate. This illustrates the need for very small changes as specified by Darwin.

Many biologists in Darwin's time argued that almost all organisms could be divided into distinct groups and that the fossil record had failed to provide examples of intermediate forms. Darwin responded that the fossil record was incomplete and that thousands of intermediates would be discovered, but to date his prediction has proved incorrect. The story of Charles D Walcott illustrates both the facts about the fossil record and the hold that evolution has on the scientific community.[5,6] Walcott was exploring the Burgess Pass in British Columbia when he discovered a rich source of fossils preserved in the fine mud. This fine mud preserved not just the skeletons of the animals it trapped but the soft outer tissue and the inner organs. What he discovered in this amazing, natural museum was animals with the basic anatomies of all the animals alive today. This result was completely unexpected because evolution theory suggested that there should be a gradual appearance of more complex animals, but what Walcott had revealed was that animals with fully formed eyes, gills, jointed limbs and intestines all appeared during a period of a few million years between 500 and 600 million years ago. This became known as the "Cambrian Explosion," because the changes observed were much greater in magnitude than would be expected in such a short time by Darwin's gradual evolution theory. Walcott was a world renowned paleontologist and he clearly realized that what he had found could be very damaging to the theory of evolution. He excavated sixty thousand fossils, shipped them to the Smithsonian Institution in Washington DC, where he was a Director, and carefully stored them with complete records, but did not write any papers proclaiming his historic discovery. Walcott's excavations took place at the opening of the 20th century, but it was about eighty years before these fossils were rediscovered, eighty years when vital evidence against evolution remained hidden allowing generations to grow up believing evolution to be unchallenged.

So let us recap what this treasure trove of fossils revealed. Despite the vast number of creatures preserved in almost perfect condition, no evidence of the predicted thousands of intermediate links between phyla were found. New animals with complex organs were shown to appear suddenly in the fossil record, not gradually as Darwin predicted. These results have been confirmed in other excavations around the world in which many previously unknown forms of life have been discovered, but none of the intermediate forms as predicted by Darwin. These results have shown that the Cambrian explosion resulted in all the phyla that exist today, together with some others that have become extinct. It is not possible to say what caused Walcott to withhold the information he had, but it is clear that he was a believer in Darwin's evolution and was aware of the grip this theory had on the academic world. When I asked the senior lecturer in biology mentioned at the start of this chapter what would be the reaction in her college if she argued against evolution, she replied, "it would be academic suicide." Universities allow all sorts of outlandish views to be held by their staff knowing that every so often these views will lead to breakthroughs, but atheists regard evolution as giving their view of life intellectual respectability, so they defend it with religious fervor against all opposition, irrespective of the facts.

One of the difficulties for the student is to reconcile the fact that there are no fossils of intermediate types with sketches of such creatures that appear in books on evolution. When Darwin acknowledged the lack of intermediates he suggested that his readers use their imaginations to fill in the gaps. This may have had some validity when the fossil record was sparse but it has less justification after exhaustive excavations have failed to produce any evidence of their existence. Examples found in textbooks include a steady change from a quadruped primate similar to an orangutan through an increasingly erect progression to a bipedal primate like man. No evidence has been found of the intermediate stages.

The problem was summarized by the paleontologist Niles Eldridge as follows: "No wonder paleontologists have shied away from evolution for so long. It never seems to happen. Assiduous collecting up cliff faces yields zigzags, minor oscillations and very slight accumulations of change – over millions of years, at a rate too slow to account for all the prodigious change that has occurred in evolutionary history. When we do see the introduction of evolutionary novelty it usually shows up with a bang, and often with no firm evidence that the fossils did not evolve elsewhere! Evolution cannot be forever going on somewhere else. Yet that's how the fossil record has struck many a forlorn paleontologist looking to learn something about evolution."[7] As a result of their observations Eldridge and Gould proposed a theory they called "punctuated equilibrium" that proposed that the fossil record of long periods of stability interspersed with periods of rapid change represented the true path of evolution. The suggestion was that in small isolated populations any changes, once they occurred, could sweep through the whole population very quickly. The problem with the new theory is that the rate at which mutations take place is proportional to the size of the population. Therefore in a small population it would take much longer for any useful mutation to occur so there is, on average, not a great advantage to considering a small group. This modification to Darwin's theory has been opposed by traditional neo Darwinists who have dubbed it evolution by jerks. This insult has been rebuffed by the revisionists who call the traditional theory evolution by creeps.[8] The fact that paleontology reveals that most species remain virtually unchanged for long periods of time and then change suddenly, is completely ignored by most evolutionary biologists. This factual evidence is quite contrary to the gradual theory of Darwin that has been portrayed as unchallenged by popular television programs for 50 years. It appears that program producers have no intention of letting their viewers entertain any doubts that the theory that popular scientists have presented for so long has serious problems. As S.J.Gould, a champion of the punctuated equilibrium theory admits, "Every paleontologist knows that most species don't change....They may get a little bigger or bumpier. But they remain the same species and that's not due to imperfection and gaps but stasis. And yet this remarkable stasis has generally been ignored as no data. If they don't change, its not evolution so you don't talk about it."[9]

The fact that the fossil record reveals very few intermediate steps is not the only reason to doubt Darwin's evolution. Atheist evolutionists would have us believe that birds evolved from amphibians by chance mutations. Amphibians have a respiratory system in which air enters the lungs and exits through the same tubes, in a manner similar to our own. Birds have a unique respiratory system in which air passes directly through the lungs. In this unique system the lung is fixed rigidly to the body wall and cannot expand in volume like the amphibian lung. It can only exist because of a number of unique adaptations that are beyond the scope of this book.[10] It is vital that both birds and amphibians have a regular efficient supply of oxygen and it is, so far, beyond the imagination of any biologist to describe a series of small changes that would lead from the amphibian respiratory system to the system in all birds, with intermediate systems that are at least as efficient as those they replaced. Bird experts believe that the higher efficiency of the avian respiratory system allows birds to fly at great altitudes where climbers have great difficulty in surviving without an oxygen supply.[11] But Darwin's step by step evolution would surely have produced a bird from amphibians with an amphibian type lung, that could have found a survival niche. The ability to fly when no other creatures were able to would surely have provided a survival advantage. It would seem to require a designer who knew that it would be advantageous for some birds to fly at a great height to have the foresight to supply a completely novel respiratory system for the purpose.

Among the many examples that point to utility far beyond the basic functioning that evolution would have produced, Michael Denton[12] highlights the example of the human brain, that has much greater capability than that which would be required for survival. Music and art and all artistic creations are unnecessary distractions for the hominid we are supposed to have evolved from, whose every waking moment should have been concerned with safety from predators and finding food. Indeed the ability to contemplate the future, whether the ultimate fate of the earth is to be destroyed by the eventual exhaustion of the sun, or by collision with a meteor, seems to be something to take our minds off vital day to day survival. The fact that we have free time now to philosophize, when the early man depicted by evolution would not, argues greatly that the brain was designed with the ability for abstract thought ready for us to use it when we had the time to do so. The hunter gatherer who spent his days wondering what the distant future held for him would hardly be in as good a position to survive as the one who got on with finding the necessary food to keep his family alive. The mathematician Roger Penrose tells us that he believes in natural selection but he also studied the nature of consciousness, giving special consideration to mathematical algorithms. Algorithms are a series of logical steps that can be followed to solve a problem. Professor Penrose concludes that the ability that a programmer has to produce these algorithms may have evolved, but the ability to judge whether the program will actually work is not an algorithmic process. He then states that "things at least seem to organize themselves somewhat better than they 'ought' to, just on the basis of blind-chance evolution and natural selection." [13]

The next thing we must consider is the basic unit of life, the cell. It was common in Darwin's time to think of the simple cell as a homogeneous globule of protoplasm deserving the description simple. It was not difficult for early evolutionists to imagine this simple cell being produced by chance in a pond of muddy water. The reality is very much more complex. By 1953 it was known that the cell was made of proteins that were in turn made of amino acids. When Stanley Miller synthesized amino acids by passing electric currents at high voltage through a mixture of inorganic chemicals that were thought to represent a possible pre-life muddy pool, evolutionists believed they were well on the way to showing how life started and would soon be able to create living cells from inorganic compounds. It was soon shown however that proteins in the cell are made of chains of up to three thousand amino acids in precise orders, and although many attempts have been made to create these proteins from amino acids in the ideal conditions of the laboratory they have all been unsuccessful.[14] If a complex technique to create proteins from amino acids is developed in the future, it will not provide a convincing case for the natural formation of proteins. The cell, in the ultimate chicken and egg situation, has no trouble making proteins but it uses proteins to do so. The simplest self contained cell is called a prokaryotic cell[15], and it has a nucleoid containing its DNA that works together with many specialized proteins, like a small, well designed factory. It has mobility provided by one or more flagella, that we will discuss later, and is surrounded by a cell wall that selectively lets nutrients in and waste products out as required. The cell wall also protects the cell from the surrounding fluids whilst holding the cell together.

DNA is made up of a long string of sub units called nucleotides. Each nucleotide consists of a sugar, a nitrogen-containing base and a phosphate group. There are four nucleotides occurring in DNA and their differences are found in the structure of their bases. The bases are commonly identified by the first letter of their chemical names: A,C,G, and T (Adenine, Cytosine, Guanine and Thymine). DNA is arranged as a double helix with two identical halves held together by hydrogen bonds between pairs of nitrogenous bases. The hydrogen bonds are between an A base in one helix and a T base in the second helix or between a C base in one helix and a G base in the second forming what are called 'base pairs'. There are about 3×10^9 base pairs in the human genome and only about 1.5% of them make up the approximately 23000 protein-coding genes. These genes act as a template containing all the information required to produce every specialized protein in the cell. DNA can be thought of as the instruction code that controls all the functions of a cell just as the list of instructions in a computer program controls the actions of the computer. Each individual instruction is known as a gene and each gene is made up of a combination of many letters in the DNA. The DNA can be copied by splitting into two identical halves and using each half as the template for the production of a new one. (a more recent model describes the DNA as equivalent to a computer's hardware and he epigenomes which activate individual genes as the software)

Outside the nucleoid, specialized proteins within the cell provide energy, remove waste and transport newly created proteins to precisely where they are required. All this complex molecular structure and control, that is common to the cells in all living things, takes place without any outside direction being necessary. Although many biology textbooks still suggest that the simple cell arose from some pre-biotic slime, many atheist biologists acknowledge that the possibility of such a complex living system coming together by chance on earth is remote. This leads such authorities as Francis Crick, a co-discoverer of the structure of DNA, to suggest that life on earth was seeded from outer space,[16] although this still fails to answer the question of how life was created. It is clear that we would not be able to tell the difference between life from outer space and life created by God, but great effort is being made to search nearby heavenly bodies and passing space debris for signs of life. For decades sensitive radio receivers have been scanning the heavens with the same mission, to find intelligent life and eliminate the idea of God the creator.

Let us try to get a feel for the probability that the proteins required for life came together by chance. Humans together with a wide range of creatures possess about 23,000 genes within their DNA with which to produce the proteins that support life.[17] There are estimated to be approximately 30 million species known on earth but let us assume many unknown species exist, so we will work with the number 50 million species. If they all have 23000 genes and assume there is no commonality between genes (in order to give us a maximum estimate), life exhibits a maximum of 23x50 billion or $1.15x10^{12}$ genes and a possible maximum of $1.15x10^{12}$ proteins produced by them.[18] The proteins produced are each made up of between about 50 to more than 3000 amino acids. Although more than 100 amino acids occur in living organisms only 20 varieties of amino acid are commonly used as building blocks for proteins. If we take a typical protein with about 200 amino acids how many different combinations are possible using 20 amino acids? This math is very simple. There are 20 possibilities for the first choice 20 for the second and so on so there are 20x20x20....x20 with 200 twenties as possibilities. That's $1.6x10^{260}$, a colossal number. Out of this number of possible amino acid combinations a maximum of only $1.15x10^{12}$ have been selected "by chance" for life. (This number would be considerably smaller if we reduced it to account for genes that are common to more than one species.) That's about one in $1.4x10^{248}$, a proportion so small that it can safely be regarded as almost zero. If this calculation were repeated considering not just the 20 amino acids used in living cells but including all the more than 100 known amino acids, the possibility of all the proteins present in the simple cell being formed together by chance is even more remote. There are two problems that arise from these results. There are a vast number of possible amino acid combinations of which only a tiny proportion are found as proteins in living creatures. The first problem is how did a random process result in sufficient of these proteins to form in one location so that even the simplest living things could be created? If the atheist argues that there are many more possible phyla capable of being evolved out of other combinations of amino acids and existing living things were formed from the amino acids that just happened to come together first, why have no new life forms evolved using a different set of proteins in the billions of years since then? If a billion different combinations of the 100 amino acids had by chance united every second for the last 3 billion years or so, while the conditions on earth enabled simple life to be supported, about $9.5x \ 10^{25}$ potential proteins would have had the possibility of being formed. That is a tiny fraction of all possible proteins, so there would be almost zero probability that any of the proteins found in living things would have been created. The probability that two or more such proteins were created in close proximity is negligible. In fact the amino acids would only exist for short periods of time after their creation by some energetic natural event such as a lightning strike or a volcano,[19] and only a minute fraction of the possible combinations could have combined. The other fact is that life was formed at around the time that the earth became able to support life not billions of years later. The probability of creating just one of the proteins present in living cells by chance is small. The probability that sufficient of the specialized proteins that are able to form a self replicating living cell were created at the same place, came together by chance and were protected immediately with a membrane, through which they could feed and remove waste, is too small to be taken seriously. It has to be concluded that seeding of life from outer space is much more likely than creation by blind chance.

It should be noted that some atheists take a rather novel approach to probability. The problem of linking random amino acids to form the proteins used in life is rather like the proverbial monkey hitting random letters on the keyboard and producing a sentence from Shakespeare. It would be easy enough to write a computer program using its random number generator to produce letters at random and look for sequences that form a word or a paragraph. You can leave such a program running continuously and only occasionally will you get an English word with more than 4 letters. Any short sentence will be very rare and looking for a given phrase from Shakespeare would be effectively impossible. This is precisely the problem facing biologists who believe random collisions of amino acids in a primeval soup produced life, because only a very small proportion of the possible combinations of amino acids form the proteins used in living cells. In just the same way when letters are strung together at random there are so many more combinations that are nonsense than combinations that form meaningful sentences. So the evangelical atheist Richard Dawkins[20] set his computer to produce a sentence from Shakespeare and compared it to the actual sentence stored in the computer to prove random change can be creative. If that was all he had done it would have been representative of the problem, but having produced a random sentence of the correct length he programmed the computer to compare it with the target phrase. He had the computer continue to copy the phrase making random changes but retaining the version that was closest to the original. In practice any letters that were correct in each comparison were retained. So he quickly arrived at an accurate copy of the target phrase. To show how this distorts the idea of random change, assume someone steals your ATM card knowing you have a six digit numerical pin number. There are a million possible numbers for the thief to try and if the ATM machine let him try repeatedly he would need to try half a million numbers to have a fifty percent chance of getting it right. If he could enter two numbers every minute it would take him almost 6 months of continuous guesswork for a 50% chance of getting your money. If the ATM generously remembered any numbers that were entered correctly however, it would be a simple matter to enter all the zeros followed by all the ones until after ten entries taking 5 minutes the thief would have 100% certainty of drawing from your account. The only way evolution could take such a sure footed path to a desired goal is if some being knew what the answer should be and made sure the correct path was followed. Now Dawkins complains that scientists who have criticized his calculation simply do not understand that this is the way things are in biology. But in the case of the emergence of life on the cooling earth there is no such thing as biology. There is only chemistry and probability, no "selfish gene" or "force of evolution" to speed things along. To be fair to Dawkins he is applying this computer calculation to hemoglobin, but even then to get any advantage each intermediate product would have to provide a survival advantage. His computer program simply kept any change that was compatible with the final sentence, the most optimistic outcome possible. Dawkins gets round the question of the start of life by postulating some as yet unknown simple self-replicating chemical that becomes more and more complex. Eventually it develops into a living cell, evolving so quickly that living cells are fully formed almost as soon as conditions on earth can support life. This theory has no facts to support it and suffers from the fact that each increase in complexity would represent a decrease in entropy, swimming upstream against the natural flow. Without a skin to protect it the chemical would soon break down in the surrounding fluid. With a simple skin to protect it the chemical would be isolated from further change. The result would be that the newly formed compound would be much more likely to decay than to survive long enough to become yet more complex. Living cells are able to produce complex compounds but they can achieve this only because they work in a highly protected environment within the cell and are equipped with a range of specialized catalysts. The cell wall that gives cells their protection is a complex construction through which the cell can absorb nutrients and remove waste products.

I want to make it clear that I do accept some of the arguments for selection. An animal whose sight improved due to a mutation so that it could see slightly more obscure sources of food would have an advantage that could cause an improved survival, that could result in evolution by natural selection. However a creature with very poor sight at the start of the supposed evolution of the eye, with say 1% of our clarity of vision, would be unable to decide if the approaching shadow was its next meal or a predator. I do not accept Dawkins' argument that a small improvement in sight at this level would provide any selection advantage, much less the massive survival bias that he implies in his computer program. The animal with such poor sight could still avoid obstructions but not much more. It would seem to me to be a more realistic model for eye development to acknowledge that there would be periods in the development when a small change resulted in real selection advantage, but there would be long periods when only a large step improvement would have this effect. Waiting for large changes takes us back to the long times demanded by the laws of probability. The fossil record shows that animals with complete eyes appear suddenly, without the many step improvements required by natural selection theories. It is also worth noting that in the unique developments such as design of the birds lung it would appear that there would need to be many intermediate lung configurations that gave no advantage over a primitive bird with an amphibian lung. In such a case change would be governed by the strict laws of probability.

Dr. Schroeder tells us that on several occasions, starting with the Wistar Institute symposium in 1967, mathematicians and biologists have got together to try to get statistical support for evolution by random mutations. The mathematics shows the probabilities to be effectively zero, so the biologists say the mathematics must be wrong because they know that is what happened.[21] Some biologists then make simplifications, putting the answer they wish for in the computer, to "prove" what they believe, then some of them use the result to "prove" that there is no God.

Darwin stated that "If it could be demonstrated that any complex organ existed that could not possibly have been created by numerous, successive slight modifications, my theory would absolutely break down." Professor Michael Behe[22] has shown several examples drawn from his specialty of microbiology where gradual development is difficult to conceive. These break down into three main types. Firstly the chicken and egg situation. As mentioned above the simplest independent cell is made up of many complex proteins that are synthesized by the cell using proteins. There are many different proteins in the simple cell that perform functions that are essential to its survival, but the only known source of these proteins is the cell itself. Secondly there are organs that Behe describes as being irreducibly complex. Among the examples described by Behe is the cilium, a whip like structure that has the ability to flex and enable cells to move. Cilia provide the mobility for prokryatic cells, so they are fully formed on some of the earliest of living creations. A cilium consists of a number of parts that microbiologists have been able to remove individually. They have found that the removal of any one of the constituent parts effectively paralyses the cilium, making it as useless as a mousetrap without one of its parts. A step by step development of the cilium would produce organisms of no value and would violate Darwin's criterion.

Michael Behe also describes mechanisms in the body that require many specialized components to work in sequence. One of his examples is the blood clotting sequence in mammals. The blood is circulated under pressure in a closed system and any puncture of the of veins or arteries could result in the loss of the entire blood supply in the body unless swift action is taken. The blood clotting system is automatically undertaken by a number of highly specialized proteins that are present in the blood at all times. Fibrinogen, that forms the clot, is a molecule shaped like a barbell with an extra spherical bump at its center. When a cut causes bleeding another protein called thrombin slices off small pieces of the fibrinogen leaving sticky patches on the freshly exposed surfaces. The modified molecule is called fibrin. The sticky patches on the fibrin molecules enable them to stick together and form a series of long threads that cross over each other and form a thin patch that covers the wound. Now thrombin cannot go chopping ends off fibrinogen without good reason or it would cause a blood clot and stop the flow of blood, so it has to be initiated by a series of enzymes whose action results in activation of the fibrinogen only when and where the cut has been detected. The process of locating the cut and activating the fibrinogen in the correct amount at the right location is a complex process involving more than ten specialized proteins and enzymes working in the correct sequence without any active thought by the injured animal. As Behe points out this is only half the problem, because if the blood continues to add to the clot it will prevent blood from flowing, that could be just as injurious to the animal as the original cut without a blood clotting mechanism. So after the clot has staunched the blood flow, all the active molecules must be turned off and the blood returned to normal. As an electronics engineer I designed a number of event-driven logic systems,[23] in which a detector waits for a specific condition to be met before initiating an action. This leads to a further condition, in time, that is detected, in turn, to produce a further action. Let us consider a simple situation of an automatic barrier to stop automobiles from crossing a railway when a train is passing. The minimum requirements are a system for detecting the approaching train, that must operate lights and audible warning systems at the crossing, well before the train arrives. A second detector, closer to the crossing than the first detector, must activate a mechanism to lower the gates to stop traffic from crossing the line. A further detector after the crossing sends a signal to indicate that the train has passed the crossing and this must activate a mechanism to raise the barrier and switch off the warning alarms. This system would be useless or cause chaos without all parts in place and working in the correct sequence; it is well known that imperfect systems have resulted in tragedy. The blood clotting system is just such an event driven system with many more complex steps that must be activated at precisely the correct time and that relies on many specialized components being available.

Critics of Darwin pointed out the problem of partial development. How could a wing be of any use when only 10% developed and what would cause it to survive, much less continue in development to become a complete wing? As Gould points out, this argument assumed functional continuity.[24] Darwin countered this criticism with the suggestion that wings, for example, originally had other uses and they developed for those uses until they became usable as wings. As a result of this proposition we find various suggestions about the evolution of wings as nets to catch insects, for example, although as Denton[25] points out the characteristics of the two functions are very different. A limb that could catch an insect and feed it to the mouth of an animal would be too useful to adapt through an intermediate stage where it could not support flight nor catch insects. A second suggestion is that a hard protrusion from the scale of an amphibian would slow down its descent when it jumped from a tree, thereby enabling it to jump from greater heights. Clearly such a protrusion would be most effective if it were stiff and it would no longer have this slowing down effect if it became soft and fluffy like a bird's wing. The wing only works because it is made of parallel filaments that interlock with hooks and barbules. The steps required to develop the birds wing from a stiff piece of a reptile's scale would certainly go through intermediate stages in which the animal was unable to fly but the soft wing no longer slowed it down as effectively as its stiff predecessor. The principle of functional change with structural continuity that Darwin proposed is another use of imagination to support development by chance and is completely without proof, allowing the committed evolutionist to invent a new suggested use for a partially developed organ whenever an earlier suggestion is proved to be implausible. It is much more difficult to support an argument that a dozen or so specially developed cells, that work together in sequence to perform an essential function such as blood clotting, could all have happened to be available, fulfilling other undetermined functions, when the need for blood clotting arose. It is equally difficult to imagine a system that was partly complete and remained in that state to be completed by a chance mutation. The evolutionist's answer to Behe's blood clotting problem, is that the earliest blood circulation systems operated at low pressure and as blood pressure increased the blood clotting system grew with it "driven by the force of evolution". But the "force of evolution" once again seems rather Lamarkian, as if the need ensured that it would be met. In fact the need has to wait for a chance mutation to provide a survival advantage and useful chance mutations do not often occur. Mutations are rarely advantageous, in fact they are usually detrimental, so many generations would need to survive with incomplete blood clotting systems that would provide little or no survival advantage.

If there is no God, changes due to mutations are completely without direction and the wait for a needed change would normally be very long. Indeed, a mutation that resulted in the first step towards an improvement, but that did not result in a significant increased ability to survive on its own, would have a real probability of mutating again before the mutation to cause the second step occured.[26]

We must now look at how the theory of evolution affects the faith of different groups of people. The first group to consider are the atheists. Atheists have no choice but to believe that there is a completely natural cause for everything, including life, and they will continue to work hard to explain all the problems in a natural way. This is perfectly consistent with their beliefs but they go too far when they claim to have proved that all creation has a completely natural explanation, after using their imaginations to make up for any shortcomings in their theories, and then extrapolate to say that this proves there is no God. [27] Atheists have the task of explaining the creation of the

Universe from nothing. when all experimental evidence suggests mass/energy is conserved and entropy always increases.

Christians can roughly be divided into three groups. There are Christians who accept one of the forms of naturalistic evolution as the sole way in which God performed creation. One member of this group, Dr. Francis Collins, head of the human genome project, has fully expressed his views in print.[28] Collins describes himself as a theist and describes one of his beliefs being that "once evolution got underway, no special supernatural intervention was required." If this were proved beyond doubt we would have to accept it as fact, but to accept it as a precondition of study seems to be rather like tying God's hands behind his back. Since the Christian believes that God intervened in human affairs to correct the problem of sin when Christ was born, it seems rather high handed to postulate that he could not intervene in the process of animal development.

The second group of Christians take the view that the whole of creation was completed in 6 days which leads them to dispute all the results that science supports about the age of the universe and the earth. This group of people have produced a wide range of literature to support their view.[29] There are a number of reasons why I find the creationist view difficult to support. For example the distances to the stars are known and are measured in light years. Some of them are many millions of light years away and yet the light from them reaches us. If God created them in situ in the recent past we would be observing new stars appearing as their light reached us. Now it is possible that God created them 6000 years ago and at the same time created light around them as if they had been shining for millions of years. This would mean that everything we see in the distant universe is an illusion because the light that is apparently created by distant heavenly bodies is a separate creation. It is difficult enough to understand why God would create such a deception, but a further problem arose in 1987 when an astronomer in Chile observed a star exploding in the night sky. The star was well known to astronomers and its distance from the earth had been determined to be about 163,000 light years away.[30] If God had created that star only 6000 years ago he would have had to create the illusion of its violent demise to reach us in 1987. It would be difficult to imagine a reason for God to create such an illusion unless he wanted to deceive us, which I find hard to believe. A second experimental check on the age of the earth is provided by scientists working at the south pole who drive tubes into the ice and draw them out to examine them. They reveal a series of bands, one for each year, that show the depth of ice accumulated each year. These investigations show a history of greater than 6000 years and cannot be disputed in the way that radioactive dating methods have been.

The third group of people believe that creation is the result of intelligent design. They believe, as I do, that scientists are capable of producing accurate measurements and the fact that scientists publish their work and others can check it means that, in the long run, correct results are obtained. Michael Behe who is a professor of biology at Lehigh University in the U.S.A is one of the leading proponents of "intelligent design" and he believes that the examples he has discussed such as the multiple steps required in blood clotting show that evolution alone cannot account for all the complexity we find in living things. Christian followers of ID would say that scientists can obtain accurate data, but when it comes to theorizing about those results, there are occasions where an atheistic belief will lead to totally incorrect conclusions. The continuous creation theory of the universe was a recent example where atheist philosophy propelled the theory to a position of greater acceptance than it deserved. The Bible is very clear that God created time and space and the current, accepted, creation science supports that view. I take the view that when the facts of science in other fields are fully known there will be no conflict with the teachings of the Bible, but we must be clear about scientific facts and also about what the Bible really says.

We must now look at the mechanism of mutation in a little more detail. A mutation is a permanent change in the DNA base sequence. It may have no apparent effect on the organism. Occasionally it may have a beneficial effect but it is far more likely to be detrimental to the organism. The most common mutation is called base substitution that, as its name suggests, is the result of one nitrogenous base in the DNA code being incorrect. But organisms have a variety of mechanisms for repairing copying errors, often by removing them with enzymes, then replacing the correct nucleotide. The repair mechanism does not always work: for example sickle cell anemia occurs when both parents have a single base substitution in their DNA code. The fact that both carriers of the sickle cell mutation may suffer no ill effects illustrates the fact that a mutation may have no effect on the second generation if only one parent has it. If a beneficial mutation occurs it has to spread throughout the whole population, that will take many generations, but for mutations to pass from one generation to the next they must take place in the germ cells or gametes (i.e.eggs or sperm). The accepted rate of mutations in the human gamete is about four per 100,000 generations.[31] Of the 3.1 billion base pairs in the human genome only 1.5% are used for protein production or about 45 million base pairs.[32] If a series of mutations is required before beneficial effects are produced one of the genes may be changed again before the series is complete. In fact, at the point where half the number of mutations required to make an advantageous change have occurred, the next mutation is just as likely to occur in the already changed cells as in the unchanged ones. The time required for a series of truly random mutations to produce the massive changes from the single cell to the wide range of creatures found on earth is longer than the time available, if strict probability rules are followed. So atheist evolutionists, like to assume optimistic pathways in which every advantageous mutation is retained. Further, the probability of complex systems such as the eye developing by chance in the short period revealed by the fossil record is extremely small. But there is one further point made by Schroeder.[33] If we accept that the long sequence of chance mutations that result in an eye has an extremely low probability, the atheist must accept that it may not have happened. We could possibly have had infra red vision like the rattle snake, or sonic detection like the bat, but let us say that despite the low probability chance did provide us with eyes with an adjustable lens and optic nerves feeding a brain that could decode the information. Now in the case of the eye, we find an almost identical structure in the primate eye and the eye of the octopus, although evolutionists believe that they developed independently by random mutations. The probability of two long sequences of independent events both occurring is equal to the product of the probability of each of the events.[34] If it is accepted that the probability of an eye developing in a specific way is very small, the probability of almost identical eyes developing independently becomes infinitesimally small and it becomes an act of great faith to believe that two such developments could have occurred by chance.

Chapter 6

Genesis and Science

The Bible opens with the words "In the beginning God created the heavens and the earth." This statement gives great irritation to the committed atheist. For many years it was accepted that the universe was stable, a situation that both the atheist, who believed that the universe had always been the same, and the Christian, who believed that the universe was unchanged since creation by God, could accept. When Einstein was considering the implications of his General Relativity Equations he realized that their solution implied an expanding universe. Einstein accepted the general belief that the Universe was stable and added an "hypothetical term" to his field equations to make them consistent with a stable universe,[1] an action that he later regarded as the greatest blunder of his life.[2] In 1868 Sir William Huggins observed a slight shift towards the red end of the spectrum in the dark lines in the spectra of some bright stars. He used the Doppler effect to show that the shift could be the result of a change in the wavelength of the light from the stars, caused by the stars' motion away from the earth. Further observations by Vesto Melvin Slipher confirmed that the majority of visible nebulae are moving away from earth. In the 1920s the astronomer Edwin Hubble showed that the speed at which galaxies are moving away from us is approximately proportional to the distance that separates us.[3] This led to the suggestion that there had been an origin, and a moment of creation, when all matter had been projected outwards, an event that eventually became part of what is known as "the big bang theory."

The atheist does not want to endorse any theory that suggests a time of creation because that points to a creator. The prominent atheist, John Maddox, who was the editor of the science magazine "Nature," said that "the big bang theory is philosophically unacceptable" [4] and other leading scientists agreed with him. So attempts were made to make the fact of an expanding universe fit into an acceptable atheist philosophy. One such hypothesis was the Continuous Creation Theory associated with Professor Hoyle of Cambridge, who proposed that hydrogen was continuously being created throughout space, thereby feeding its continuous expansion. This theory died because it was not supported by observational evidence. The other main theory was the Continuous Oscillation Theory that suggested that the gravitational attraction within the universe would slow down its expansion replacing it with contraction and eventually lead to its collapse. The cycle would then start again with a further "big bang". For this to satisfy atheistic beliefs the expansion and contraction of the universe would need to be a continuous phenomenon that had occurred an infinite number of times. It was shown that if this theory was correct, each successive cycle would result in more photons and less matter, with the result that the present universe would be material free, that is clearly not the case.[5]

In about 1961, when I was reading physics at Manchester University, I attended a lecture on cosmology by Professor Sir Bernard Lovell, who was at the time the most distinguished radio astronomer. Sir Bernard was responsible for establishing the world's first large steerable radio telescope at Jodrell Bank. He concluded the lecture with his new discovery that radio stars were moving away from us, reinforcing the earlier work that had shown the visible universe to be expanding. Sir Bernard discussed all the then current theories including the work of Bondi, Gold and Hoyle, but I left the lecture with the impression that he accepted the Big Bang Theory as the most acceptable, rather against the trend of popular science at the time, and I found it theologically fine. It seems to fit with the many verses like Isaiah 40:22, that tells of a God who "stretches out the heavens like a curtain and spreads them out like a tent to dwell in."

Today the Big Bang Theory is almost universally accepted by astronomers, so they have caught up with the idea that time and space had a beginning just as Genesis tells us. If God created the universe from nothing there will be a first creation event. This may turn out to be before the big bang, in preparation for it, but there will have been an initial event. It will be impossible to determine the conditions that existed before this event, a situation that will continue to be a natural irritation to the scientist who, not unreasonably, wants to explain everything with a continuum of natural events. We must expect atheists to work hard to produce theories that speculate how the creative act may have occurred naturally, with support from the popular science media that will promote these theories as if they are proved.

It is worth noting at this point that the word for creation appears in Genesis chapter 1 only in verses 1, 21 and 27.[6] Its first use in chapter 1 clearly tells us that God created the universe from nothing and that the initial act was sufficient to give direction to its development. So the resulting universe, including the planet earth, with its ability to support life, were all designed into that creative act. It is difficult to give a line by line commentary on this chapter without knowing what the original language meant to Moses. Berishis' commentary written about a thousand years ago, before today's conflict between Genesis and Science, says of verse one that it "does not intend to teach the order of creation."[7] The commentary then goes on to state how the verse would have been worded if the order of creation had been intended. It is my intention therefore to examine parts of the chapter where the meaning is clear and see if they are in agreement with science. I acknowledge that Genesis is not a science textbook and we should not expect too much detail in this short account, but if it is the inspired word of God I do not want to treat it as irrelevant.

The first verse of Genesis chapter 1 tells us that in the beginning God created the heavens and the earth and the following verses tell us that he did it over time. It also tells us a few facts about the steps in creation but not necessarily in their exact sequence. The creative act required an immense amount of power and the Bible tells us that God can produce this power with his word. Hebrews chapter 4 verse 12 tells us that the word of God is quick and powerful. The Gospel of John tells us that the word through which God expressed himself in the beginning was Jesus Christ.[8] So through Jesus, God produced the power required for creation.

The second verse of Genesis chapter 1 states **"and the earth was without form and void; and darkness was upon the face of the deep."**

This clearly does not describe an earth that was fully formed like it is today. Today the earth has a very definite shape that is almost spherical. If, in the beginning, God created all matter in one place, as science suggests, then the earth, in that initial creation, would be mixed up with all the other matter, so it would be completely without any recognizable shape.

Verse three of Genesis 1 says **"And God said let there be light; and there was light."** The accepted composition of the early universe would have included a mixture of particles of matter and antimatter greatly outnumbered by high energy photons. Wienberg states that "it was light that formed the dominant constituent" of the early universe.[9] The particles of matter that remained after the majority of them had been annihilated by combining with particles of antimatter eventually became every solid thing we see, including the earth. So the earth was completely mixed up with light in this early creation.

Verse 5 of Genesis 1 says **"So the evening and the morning were the first day"** Why does the Bible say the evening and the morning were the first day? Surely we would expect that the morning and the evening bounded the first day. And surely there is no earth and sun in the beginning, so how would we get an evening and morning? I am grateful for the writings of the Hebrew scholar Dr. Schroeder for illumination at several points in this chapter.[10] Firstly he points out that the Old Testament concept of a day starts with the evening, so in Leviticus[11] we read "from evening to evening you shall celebrate your Sabbath." But verse 5 of Genesis says evening to morning which is not even an Old Testament day. Schroeder goes on to explain that the Hebrew word for evening implies the visual conditions in the evening, when objects are obscure and blurred so you cannot see clearly. The Hebrew for morning implies things are becoming clear and distinct. We are being told that the disorder of the early, without form and void creation is being changed step by step into a creation with the order that God has designed. So the Bible is teaching that God made the heavens and earth over a period of time and that throughout this period order was increasing. In chapter 4 we used the definition of entropy given by Encyclopedia Britannica, that describes it as a measure of the energy of a system that is not available to do work. It goes on to say that entropy is a measure of the disorder of a system. Consider an insulated bowl with two halves separated by an insulated divider. In one side of the bowl we have hot water and in the other side we have cold water. We can use this system to do work for us. For example we could make a thermocouple by taking two lengths of wire, one made of copper and the other iron, and twisting their ends together so that we have a continuous loop with two junctions. If we put one junction in the hot water and one in the cold, electrical current will flow in the wires, around the loop and we could use this to do work. The system with the hot water separated out from the cold is an organized system and therefore energy is available to do work. If we slide the divider out between the hot and cold water the hot and cold water will mix and the system will become disorganized. In an ideal system there has been no change of energy when the hot and cold water combined to form a warm mixture, but now none of this energy is able to produce current in the thermocouple wires because there is no temperature difference in the system. The system has increased in disorder and entropy, even though the total energy has not changed, so we see that we need a low entropy or ordered system in order to be able to do useful work. Moving a system from a high entropy state to a low entropy state requires the expenditure of external energy. Isolated self contained systems never move to a more ordered system with lower entropy. In creation we find that God was ensuring that the universe that we inhabit was an ordered, low entropy system. The sun is providing the energy we need to live on earth and its ability to do this is because of the order in creation.

Verses 6 to 8 of Genesis 1 say **"And God said let there be a firmament in the midst of the waters and let it divide the waters from the waters.......And God called the firmament heaven"**

My reading of these verses is that by this point the earth has been created and is revolving around the sun. The earth is hot but cooling and surrounded by a dense layer of cloud. As the cloud lifts, a firmament, or layer of gases is created between the cloud mass and the water covering the earth. In other words the air or atmosphere was formed between the water covering the earth and the still dense cloud mass above. The Bible uses the word heaven in three different ways and this one refers to our atmosphere. Verse 20 of Genesis 1 makes the meaning of heaven in this passage clear when it says that the first winged creatures fly above the earth in the open firmament of heaven.

Verse 9 of Genesis chapter 1 says **"Then God said Let the waters under the heavens be gathered together into one place and let the dry land appear."**

Geologists would agree, I think, that all the land mass has at some stage been covered with water. As the earth cooled the ice caps could form and the dry land appeared. I think it is also accepted that the continents were once connected so that there was one large land mass (or possibly two) and one large ocean, as this verse implies. It is accepted science that Africa was joined to South America for example, so the mass of land surrounded by a single ocean described by this verse is in line with scientific fact. The land would have been much flatter than it is now. As the tectonic plates have moved the continents have separated and land masses have pushed into each other, creating mountain ranges, whilst volcanic action has also changed the landscape.

Verse 11 of chapter 1 says **"Then God said let the earth bring forth grass, the herb that yields seed, and the fruit tree that yields fruit according to its kind"**

Now the Bible doesn't say that this development required any further creative act from God. The earth may have brought forth grass and trees as a result of natural evolution as it had been designed to do. Science shows that mono-cellular plant life (or algae) in the ocean was a very early form of life that appeared, but God gave this message to Moses over 3000 years ago and there was no language to describe things that can only be seen under a microscope. But it is accepted that plants had to be established in order to produce the oxygen that animals require for respiration and the early mono-cellular plants were the first step in a process that led to all the plants described in verse 11. The Bible does not say that it required another creative act for plants to be established and it is possible that in the first creative act that produced the universe, the creation of plant life was included. It is probably true to say that these early plants were created with the potential to develop into all the plants that have existed. It is generally accepted that green algae, that were part of the early life forms, can live in moist places on land and that some members of the species are believed to be linked structurally and biochemically to the plant kingdom.[12] So here we see plant life is established, and it produces the oxygen that will support animals and provide the protective ozone layer.

Now I realize that if no new creative act was required to start life it implies that in the initial creation there was included a provision for life to begin when the conditions for life were met. This suggests the possibility that there exists a mechanism or law that creates life despite the low probability of it occurring by chance. If such a law is discovered the atheist will say "you see life is just the result of natural laws," ignoring the hand of the creator.

Verse 14 "and God said let there be lights in the firmament of the heavens to divide the day from the night; and let them be for signs and seasons and for days and years."

I take the view that the sun the moon and the stars were already created and that, at this time, the cloud cover cleared sufficiently for there to be a clear sky and for the sun moon and stars to be visible. This verse does not say that anything new was created. These verses are giving the viewpoint from earth where only when the cloud cleared would the heavenly bodies appear. So in verses 15 to 18 when we are told that God also made these heavenly bodies, it is a reminder that God created everything that could be seen through the now cleared skies. Now in this verse we have no new life being mentioned but the plant life was presumably evolving as it was designed to do. When I use the word evolving in this chapter I include the ideas of change by mutation and adaptation and change because the potential for change was built into the earlier life form by design.

Verses 20,21 "and God said let the waters bring forth abundantly the moving creature that hath life and fowl that may fly above the earth in the open firmament of heaven. And God created great whales (or *Schroeder–big reptiles*) and every living creature that moveth which the waters brought forth abundantly, after their kind and every winged fowl after his kind and God saw that it was good."

This passage is a mixture of "bringing forth" and "creation." The waters bring forth abundantly, presumably fish and amphibians but birds are also brought forth. We also see God in action, creating living animals and I think this is in line with what Science has discovered. In what is called the Cambrian period, paleontologists have recognized a sudden explosion of life: all the basic phyla developed quickly from the existing multicellular life forms, not gradually, step by step as Darwin postulated. Creatures suddenly appear in the fossil record with two working eyes giving them binocular vision with no evidence of gradual development. Some time later another group of creatures appear suddenly including insects with wings. This verse suggests to me that God performed separate acts of creation to produce animal groups as the environment and plant life could support them. It is clear that God did not abandon the development that had taken place in the billions of years of evolution, but developed new creatures using the existing protein building blocks and DNA structure. By this time the atmosphere had gradually changed to support more complex life forms and the basic cellular life was ready to be developed into more advanced forms. The Bible teaching that God moved to develop advanced life not only agrees with paleontology, but removes the statistical problems that arise when considering development to have taken place only by random mutations. An outline of the time line that science currently gives to development is as follows. The initial creation of the universe took place about 13.7 billion years ago and the earth was formed about 4.5 billion years ago. The oldest sedimentary rocks believed to be over 3.3 billion years old are found in North America and Africa and they have been shown to contain fossils of single celled organisms of similar shape and dimensions to microbes found today.[13] This shows that life did not have billions of years for all the combinations of amino acids to come together by chance. Soon after the earth had cooled and water was available in liquid form we find life. About 2.77 billion years go by, in which time single celled organisms have developed into multi-celled organisms. Then during a period that may have been as short as 5 million years, about 530 million years ago, massive changes occur and creatures with all the basic body shapes found today are formed. To believe that this occurred due to chance mutations defies statistics. The Bible says God made discrete changes to advance animal development, that probably included the first creatures with eyes and wings. These created phyla developed into all the animals we know today plus some that have become extinct, but no new phyla have evolved in the past 530 million years! Notice once again that the verse describes both "the waters bringing forth" and God creating as if there was God's active intervention acting together with natural development.

Verse 24 "And God said let the earth bring forth the living creature after his kind, cattle and creeping thing and the beast of the earth after his kind and it was so."

So after God's creative intervention we have more development of land animals, also breeding after their kind, insects breeding insects, mammals breeding mammals. Note that the expression " let the earth bring forth" is used here with no direct suggestion of a new creative act. There is room here for evolution although I have difficulty believing that God was playing dice with the outcome, and it may be that the possible outcomes were more tightly defined by the existing DNA than pure random mutations would suggest. Schroeder develops the concept of a latent library of genes in the early Precambrian creation. In this thesis the vast amounts of genes stored in algae, that he claims are far larger than the organism requires, are regarded as providing the building blocks for advanced organs in today's living things.[14] This concept clearly suggests the foresight of a creator.

Verses 26, 27 & Ch 2 verse 7 "And God said let us make man in our own image after our likeness" ....

"So God created man in his own image, in the image of God he created him; male and female he created them"...."and the Lord God formed man of the dust of the ground and breathed into his nostrils the breath of life; and man became a living soul"

In these verses we once again find God creating. God chose an isolated part of the earth called the Garden of Eden in which he could control the environment and the animals with which this first human family would come into contact. Here he created mankind. It seems that this separate garden area gave the human family a clean start in a non-threatening environment, away from the creatures outside. Since we share much of our DNA with other primates, it seems possible that the creation of man may have involved a step development from existing primates, similar to the creative act in the Cambrian period, but of course it could have been a new creation based on the evolved primates. But the important act in chapter 2 is that God breathed into man's nostrils a soul of life and man became a living soul in the image of God; unlike all other creatures however similar they are to us, despite the atheists' desire to classify us as just another primate. Genesis chapter 1 verse 30 tells us that all animals were given the breath of life or *nefesh* but only man was given a soul or *neshamah*. [15]

To summarize, Genesis says that :-

1) God made the Universe over a period of time.

2) God ensured that the universe was in an ordered low entropy state.

3) The initial creation was without form and void.

4) Light was an early component of creation.

5) The land on earth was at one time covered with water.

6) The water was gathered together allowing dry land to appear.

7) The early earth, that would be hot, was covered in dense cloud.

8) As the earth cooled the clouds lifted and an atmosphere was formed between the clouds and the earth.

9) Plants were established. These produced the oxygen and ozone layers that made the earth habitable.

10) The sea brought forth animal life but God intervened to progress the development of living things.

11) God created mankind giving us a soul unlike all other creatures. Our soul enables us to be aware of and to commune with God.

Genesis chapter 1 gives an outline of animal creation that is in the same order that science accepts, that is plants first then fish, birds and land animals followed by man in the only way that it could be revealed to Moses, who could not be expected to understand microscopic creatures. Is it reasonable to suppose that Moses just made the story up from his observations, which is what some believe? If I had been contemplating how an all powerful God would create, I think I would assume he could command and get instant results. The idea that the earth was without form and void in its initial created state would appear to be an unnecessary condition that must have confused readers in the past, but is in line with today's science. The periods of stasis with short periods of rapid change that is seen in the fossil record is compatible with the biblical account. Science clearly cannot comment on the described discrete changes made by God, however these changes can be used to explain the Cambrian explosion. It would not be surprising if God developed the new creations from the existing living creatures using the same replicating cell system.

Now where could Moses have got this creation story from? Stories that we know of from ancient times could hardly have given Moses his ideas. The Egyptians who educated Moses believed that there was a sea (called Nun) that was a god and out of it arose an egg, (Ra, or Re}, that was the sun. The sun, worshipped as a God, was believed to be able to make things like the Nile by simply naming them, that resulted in instant creation. Instant creation is just what one would guess if making up a creation story about an all powerful God.

The Babylonians had a story that two Gods fought; one slew the other and made the earth out of his flesh, the rocks out of his bones and teeth and the oceans out of his blood. It is beyond reason that Moses concocted Genesis 1 from the myths around him and it seems the only possibility is that he received his information by inspiration from God.[16] Later the Greeks believed that the Universe had always existed just as it is now because they saw no signs of movement in the stars and stability was a natural conclusion. This was the picture of the Universe that prevailed in scientific circles before the astronomical observations in the 1920's.

It is not possible to prove that God exists like solving an equation and writing QED underneath. But it is striking evidence that Moses could write this account that can be supported by modern science, with no source of information but divine inspiration.

Now I must say a brief word about time required for creation; 6 days or 14 billion years: which is it? Well I am only going to say it could be both. Few people were troubled by the idea of six days for creation until the science of the 19th century suggested a much older world. St. Augustine however over 1600 years ago questioned whether the days were the same as our days "since God is outside time and not bounded by it."[17]

Early in the 20th century Einstein theorized, and experiments have proved, that time is not an absolute quantity. An accurate clock on the moon runs faster than the same clock on earth because time is affected by gravity. Consider God's position at the start of creation. There is no earth and no sun and the space where the earth is now did not exist. If God put a clock (a very sturdy clock!) in the center of the mass without form and void, the gravity could have been very great ensuring that the clock would run very slowly, so that by the time earth was established a few billion years of aging in our time could correspond to a much shorter reading on God's clock. This also implies that the days recorded in Genesis would not necessarily be of equal lengths as measured on earth now. When we combine this with the fact that the Hebrew word for day can be used to describe a twenty four hour day or some other period of time, it seems too pedantic to insist on an age of only a few thousand years for the earth. For example, in Deuteronomy 31:17 God is recorded as saying *in that day* I will forsake them, not meaning a 24 hour day, but for a period bounded by events. I used to be concerned about the idea of God waiting so long for the universe to develop, but God is outside time, so a wait of billions of years is of no consequence to him. Note also that the Bible says "a thousand years in Your sight are like yesterday when it is past"[18] not to make us think that God ages a day every thousand years but to let us know that God is not affected by time as we are and his days are not like ours.

I have made it clear that not all Christians share my view of what the Bible and science teaches, but I believe this view deserves consideration. It should be noted that I am suggesting that the initial act of creation could have produced the earth with life up to the complexity of the Precambrian period without a further creative act. This implies that if a planet exists with similar characteristics to earth, life could have developed to that level, but advanced life forms would only result if God took further action. Genesis shows creation to have been a mixture of creative acts and waiting for the results of those acts to be fully realized. It is clearly possible that one of those creative acts was required to initiate life in which case other life in the universe will only be found if further creative acts have taken place on other planets.

Summary

It is easy to see why biologists both Christian and atheist believe in evolution. They see a continuity in the DNA of animals and humans. The same gene sequences found as codes for protein production in many animals are also found in human DNA. It seems quite reasonable to believe that God would want a system that allowed animals to adapt as conditions around them changed, and natural selection provides the means for them to do so. I believe that Genesis allows for evolution with words like "let the earth bring forth." Genesis also suggests to me that God on occasion has intervened to bring about change. Of course if God intervened he would most likely create within the framework of the existing creation. God's intervention may have been to cope with the problems that the scientists involved in intelligent design movement have identified, or it may have been to deal with problems that we have not yet uncovered. The major contribution of Genesis, that is the subject of faith and not scientific proof, is that God gave mankind a soul that enables us to commune with him. This is an ability that is unique to humans in the animal world.

The initial creation of life remains for me an open question. The atheists' suggestions of similarities between the order in cells and the order found in crystals fall short of the mark. It is easy to imagine a computer printer exhibiting a fault and printing a continuous stream of the sequence AB. Someone looking at the resulting sheet of paper covered in ABs would see order that could be regarded as the result of design, just as they see in a crystal with its regular repetition of a molecular structure. But as Professor Humphries points out[19] neither of these contain any useful information and the crystal is as far from DNA as the sheet of "ABs" is from the works of Shakespere. For me the Bible leaves the question open as to whether the initial act of creation meant that when conditions on earth were favorable life sprang forth or if God intervened to create it. The fact that God saw that the sin in the world required his intervention in the person of Jesus Christ to deal with the problem tells me that God is ready to intervene in this world's affairs at a time of his choosing. The Old Testament tells the story of the Jewish people who had made an agreement with God. The agreement called for them to behave in a certain way but they kept falling short of the mark. God often intervened and things often improved but never reached perfection. God has clearly allowed evolution to produce results that are difficult to understand but as Rees says[20] "the theory of evolution that at first seemed to remove the need for a God in the world has convincingly removed the need to explain the world's imperfections as failed outcomes of God's design." He goes on to quote from Francisco Ayala that "a major burden was removed from the shoulders of believers when convincing evidence was advanced that the design of organisms need not be attributed to the immediate agency of the creator." But that does not mean that God does not intervene at times to make corrections. When Judah and Israel failed God intervened to change their course but he did not make everything perfect.

To summarize it is possible for the Christian to believe that the whole of the natural world is the result of natural development caused by evolution. I believe however, that creative acts of God could account for apparent step changes in the animal records discovered by paleontologists and any irreducibly complex organs in creation. It should be remembered that evolutionists believe that they only have to imagine a possible path for development and that is sufficient proof. They often ignore the complex molecular changes that must accompany such development. That of course is not science, which requires experimental proof, but is an act of faith. It is however clear to me that the Genesis account of creation is compatible with evolution and for me the question is how much did God intervene.

The ultimate goal of the atheist is to demonstrate a mechanism by which everything we see around us could be created from nothing, contravening the laws of mass-energy conservation. Because this goal is a remote dream evangelical atheists have concentrated on describing evolution as a Godless process and drawn attention away from the more fundamental problem of creation itself.

Chapter 7

If I were God

Atheists dispute the existence of God in several ways, but often the criticisms boil down to "if I were God I would do things differently, and because I am so smart and so good God would have done things my way if he existed. He hasn't done things my way, therefore there is no God".

The first of these criticisms looks at the human body and says its design could be better. The critic looks at an organ such as the eye and criticizes some aspect of the design such as the existence of a blind spot and suggests ways of improving the it. The common thread connecting all such critics is that they have never designed a living organism from the ground up and seen the compromises that need to be made to actually achieve a self sustaining, living being. I spent my working life designing electronic systems to meet customers' requirements using components whose specifications were at least as well known as the workings of the human body's organs. Surprisingly the systems did not always work precisely the way I expected. I shared with many other engineers and scientists the problems of finding out what was wrong and the joy of putting it right, in the process often learning more about the components than was on the manufacturer's data sheets. I am sure that when the armchair designers made their changes to the design of the human body they would often find that they had introduced some new problems. But when we think about it, we know that God could have made us better in many ways. We could have had the eyesight of an eagle plus infra red night vision like a rattlesnake. We could have had the arm strength of a gorilla and the leg power of a kangaroo. God designed us for a purpose to meet a specification and that specification did not include our having every part made to be the best that could be achieved. With the abilities we have we have been able to dominate the animal world and exploit the natural resources that he has provided. We have developed telescopes, microscopes and night vision binoculars to improve our vision. Automobiles and aircraft travel faster than any animals and a wide range of power equipment enables us to move large masses of material anywhere on earth. Indeed, 3000 years ago, the pyramids and Stonehenge showed what an organized group of people could achieve with only their muscle and brain power. God said that man should subdue the earth[1] long before that was possible, but we can now see that our design is adequate to make that goal achievable.

The next level of criticism that the atheist aims at God is to point to the suffering in the world and say "if I were God I would not allow it." To deal with this criticism we must lay down some basic ground rules. It is clear that if there is a God he has decided to give us a degree of free will. The determinist philosophy of the 19th century argued that the future can be completely determined from a thorough knowledge of the present. It was argued that if we knew the position and velocity of every particle in the universe we would be able, knowing all the forces that act on each particle, to map the future of all matter. It was also supposed that when we had sufficient understanding of the human brain we would be able to predict all the decisions that any person would make. However experiments with small particles such as electrons revealed that the exact path of an elementary particle cannot be predicted. Two particles projected in the same direction, with the same force may travel in very different paths. In a similar manner "identical" twins brought up together and sharing similar tastes may choose different careers and lifestyles. Although some would argue that all our decisions are preprogrammed, I take it that we have a great amount of freedom in the choices we make, limited of course by natural abilities. I am not suggesting that our free will is necessarily a result of quantum physics, rather that the whole idea of pre-determinism is in doubt.

If God has decided to let us have free will how much can he intervene, when people choose to do evil, whilst letting us retain our free will? "If I were God," an atheist would say "I certainly could not watch while a child was abused." But then he is faced with a choice, should he change the abuser so that they could no longer abuse anybody or just stop them before they get started. To force them to change would remove their free will, so let us just say we disable them on the spot, paralyzing them for say one hour. This seems like a good plan so let's develop it. How about doing the same thing to abusers of old people, people who were just about to commit murder, perform cruel acts on animals, muggers, bullies in general caught just before the act? But could we limit it to stopping physical hurt once we got started? What about the slick salesmen defrauding an old lady of her life savings? An hour's paralysis before he could get her to sign the agreement, repeated every time he tried, would cure that problem. We might as well include fraudsters of all types while we are at it and reckless or drunk drivers about to start a journey that will result in death or serious injury. Paralyze them in the driving seat until they sober up or change their attitude. Clearly we should include corrupt and dishonest politicians. The oppressive dictator must be stopped but how about the politician taking bribes to vote in the interest of some rich lobbying group? Now we have a technique to put things right we might as well stop all such corruption and use it to stop cheating wives and husbands. Catch that in the bud and we could reduce agony and the spread of disease, surely a worthwhile aim. It would be difficult to estimate how many people we would be holding in a paralyzed state at any one time but it would probably amount to hundreds of millions, at least to start with. Many of the afflicted people would turn to doctors and before long the paralysis would be connected to the intended crime. The determined atheist would ascribe this to some psychological reaction of the brain before a cruel or selfish act was committed, but the conclusion that this was a limit on freedom by a God would be clear to everyone else. The result would be that people would behave almost like programmed robots and if that was what God had desired he could have made us like that in the first place.

We have similar problems when we consider illness in general. If I were God I would find it almost impossible to allow a child to be in pain. But how would I stop disease in children? If I did it in a natural way so that children were born with an all purpose-vaccine, whose potency declined with time, the medical resources of the world would strive to discover its composition so that everyone could be injected with it. The result would be eternal life for all. If I kept children free from illness in some miraculous way, that could not be revealed by scientific tests, it would almost amount to absolute proof of the existence of a God, removing free will. When considering these problems Augustine said: "since God is the highest good he would not allow any evil to exist unless his omnipotence and goodness were such as to bring good out of evil."[2] Inherent in this is the idea of what God wants for us, that may not always be what we want for ourselves. There are large numbers of people in the western world who look forward to getting drunk. I was in a local store the other day and one of the employees was telling her fellow worker that she was having difficulty with her job with the words that she had been "out drinking the night before." The implication was that she had been drinking to excess and her friend sympathized, telling her she knew how she felt. We have thousands of people whose idea of a good time is to go out and drink or take drugs until they are no longer in control of themselves. In this state they often hurt themselves or are hurt, robbed, or raped by someone taking advantage of them. The response to this varies from person to person. Some realize how foolish their behavior is and change their ways. Others continue to abuse their bodies until they do themselves irreparable harm. There are increasing numbers of people who are getting liver disease due to excessive alcohol consumption before they reach their thirtieth year. The life that God wants for us is much better than this and the pain has done some good if it causes a change in lifestyle. One aspect of this good was highlighted by C.S. Lewis when he said "God whispers to us in pleasures, speaks in our conscience, but shouts in our pains."[3] A man or woman will often continue in a life of complete self-absorption while things are going well but when things go wrong they may be brought to their knees to seek for help and guidance. A Christian friend has a son who rejected the claims of Christ and joined the army. He was sent to Afghanistan and witnessed the death and wounding of several colleagues. This brought him to realize his need to get right with God. It is surprising that God will accept us when we turn to him as a last resort, but that is a measure of his love for us.

The Old Testament tells the story of the Jewish people who entered into a voluntary agreement with God, that they would follow his laws, while for his part God agreed to look after them. For long periods of time they had peace and prosperity while they worshipped

God, but prosperity always seemed to bring with it the thought that they did not need God and they turned away from him, often putting idols in the place God should have occupied in their lives. At this point God turned away from them and let them suffer the results of their actions. The prophet Jeremiah was alive when the Israelites became slaves to the Babylonians because of their wickedness. They had sunk to the level of offering human sacrifice to false Gods, a practice that God had specifically forbidden. Jeremiah agonized over the suffering of his people so God led him into a potter's house and showed him the potter shaping the clay on his wheel. The potter was not satisfied with the way the pot was shaping up so he turned it back into a pile of clay and started again.[4] Jeremiah realized that God was not prepared to bless his people when they turned their backs on him and his ways and that, like the potter with a spoiled pot, he had to take drastic action to correct the fault. The motives of the potter are to make the very best pot that he can and the motive of God was to make the best nation that he could. So he let them suffer the consequences of their actions to bring them to their senses.

As I write this the world is facing a global financial crisis. The western world has indulged itself in a long period of living beyond its means, that banks and financial institutions, urged on by politicians, have encouraged with irresponsible lending. People who could not afford houses were lent the money to buy them, often at low initial rates that rose after a few years to monthly payments that they could not afford. Motorists who could afford a modest car, that would meet all their needs, borrowed to buy a luxury vehicle whose only contribution to their lives was to impress the neighbors and boost their egos. Governments have committed themselves to growing financial obligations without ensuring that there was sufficient revenue to pay for them, leaving massive potential debts to future generations. The British Chancellor of the Exchequer through these years was Gordon Brown and he assured the population that he had ended the years of financial crisis by following his Golden Rules, rules that now appear to have allowed far too much government spending and personal debt. Similarly lax lending rules were followed by governments and banks around the world. In the USA Treasury Secretary Henry Paulson declared that the problems in their housing market were "largely contained" in late 2007 not long before the crisis broke.[5] The general view of the world's financial leaders is that we should spend ourselves out of the crisis with even more borrowing. It goes without saying that the poor are going to suffer more than the rich. The men who encouraged customers to spend more than they could afford got large bonuses for their efforts and it is unlikely that they will be forced to repay that money. Greed has forced a crisis and the wrong people are hurt. The politicians are reluctant to make their populations reduce their consumption to the level that they can afford because it will be unpopular, but sooner or later they must face the fact that the debts must be paid if confidence in the financial system is to be restored. The Bible is very clear about the happiness that can be achieved if we are content with what we can afford, and warns us against covetousness.[6] Disobeying God's laws has consequences, just as disobeying the laws of economics or gravity does, and God wants us to learn to obey his laws because they result in more contented lives. So should God step in to put these problems right? He would have to take over the world's economies, force Governments and peoples to live within their means and in a very real sense remove free will. In the New Testament we see that God deals with us as individuals and his aim is for us to willingly become his children. He also wants the best for us. Now many people want to ignore God and hope he will leave them alone, living lives of almost complete selfish indulgence. It is not reasonable to expect that a God who loves us will be completely indifferent to how we behave. A truly loving parent whose son or daughter had been made financially independent by a grandparent's legacy would not be happy to find that they indulged in drugs and drink every night and wasted their days recovering. The loving parent would hope that their offspring would sober up and try to do something useful with their lives. The loving parent who sees their child incapable of walking in a straight line, with eyes glazed and vomit on their lips is appalled and filled with sorrow. They would do anything to change their offspring, who is in the grip of an addiction that they return to night after night. That parent would happily go through some pain to cure their child and inflict some pain if that would result in a cure. The consequences of many sins are painful, but sometimes it is this pain that turns people away from their sin to consider God's ways. Surprisingly Jesus tells us that however deep and repulsive our sinfulness, we will be accepted if we turn to him in repentance. Sinners often resent this pain and do not see themselves as others do, but many have been thankful, when they look back, for the pain that changed their lives. The slave trader John Newton went through a period of pain and hardship before he came to his senses and with the Lord's help, turned his life around. His hymn "Amazing Grace" expresses the gratitude Newton felt towards God at being saved from his old life, despite the depth of degradation that he had indulged in.

When we consider Jesus, the son of God, hanging from a cross at Calvary, it tells us about how much God loves us to allow this to happen. In some way that we cannot understand God allowed Jesus to take the punishment for all our sins so that the penalty for them could be paid, revealing to us a God who is both merciful and just. In foretelling this event, hundreds of years before Jesus was born, Isaiah said "Surely he took up our infirmities and carried our sorrows."[7] Whatever suffering we have, Jesus has experienced it, or something similar and God the father has agonized over it.

At this point we should mention another sort of pain, that which comes about by our making ourselves vulnerable to those whom we love. If we have not experienced it, we have seen the great sorrow that is caused to the innocent party when one partner in a marriage is unfaithful. There are many animals who mate with the minimum of contact and have no further connection, but we have the possibility of loving and being loved by another human being, making us vulnerable. That means there is the possibility of our being let down and hurt by another human being. God not only designed us to be like that but it is part of the way that we are in his image, for he tells us that he suffers when we sin and rebel against him. We can hear the pain as Jesus looks over Jerusalem and cries "O Jerusalem Jerusalem! You murder the prophets and stone the messengers that are sent to you. How often have I longed to gather your children around me like a bird gathering her brood together under her wings–and you would never have it."[8] God made us able to love and therefore liable to pain, a pain he shares.

There remains the problem of the relatively good person on whom great misfortune falls without any contribution from them. One of the oldest books in the Bible deals with this problem. It is the book of Job that tells the story of a good man with great wealth and a happy family. Over a short period of time he loses his wealth and his family while he is left with a painful debilitating disease. His friends are sure he must have angered God in some way and urge him to repent. Job cries out to God and for much of the book receives no answer to his cries, but he refuses to lose his trust in God. At the end of the book God speaks to him but he does not answer the question, "why has this happened to me?" He effectively tells Job that only God has the answers to the questions of why these things happen, but he is in control and although we may think he does not care he has a long term objective in view. He will balance the books in the end. When Job has absorbed this lesson he is restored to a position of health and strength once more. I would be stretching the truth if I said I was entirely satisfied with this answer, but it is clear that God puts a very high premium on our putting our faith in him to have our long term good in mind even when things look very bad.

When we consider how people lived 4000 years ago, we see people who had little in the way of medicine or pain killers. They had few ways of preserving food or storing water, so the threat of famine or drought was always with them and they had none of the modern conveniences that we consider essential. It is easy to see how people came to believe in a fearsome God who required human sacrifice to appease him but not at all easy to deduce how Abraham and his offspring came to believe that there was a God who loved them, unless we accept that he had some direct contact with this God.[9] The safety and security of one's own family must have been the major concern of all people at this time but Abraham was told that in him would all the peoples of the earth be blessed and he became convinced that God cared about him.[10] How could David write the words "the Lord is my shepherd I shall not be in want"[11] in the face of the incredible hardships that mankind faced at that time? The reason is that both Abraham and David knew the presence of God with them despite the hardships they faced and knew that God loved them.

The hardships and disasters the world faces have encouraged people with a Judeo-Christian background, who believe that God values all people, to create organizations to help people of all backgrounds and beliefs. From the Salvation Army to Christian Aid, dozens of organizations have been established to help people in need. Their message is we care because God cares and he has inspired us to help people in need from all ethnic and racial backgrounds without discrimination.

Chapter 8

The Problem with Religion

John Lennon wrote a song decrying religion. "Imagine there's no heaven" he sang "it's easy if you try." Many atheists would share his opinion of religion that they feel has caused more trouble than it is worth and to some extent I agree with them. So let us look at a popular view of religion and see how the Bible based Christianity compares with it.

Most religious people today believe that all of us fail to reach the standards of behavior that are generally accepted to be desirable and required by their God. Because we all know our own selfish nature, it is not difficult to believe that they are right. When I was at school there was supposed to be a religious instruction period every week. Few of the masters who were supposed to teach the class did anything at all, only one that I remember taught from the Bible, but one atheist teacher spent the time discussing values. The values he taught were the selfless standards of good behavior that would be common to most religions but of course there was no instruction on how to achieve these standards other than by self will.

Religion is in general about trying to please God, who is assumed to desire that we live a perfect life and the general trend has been to find ways to appease him. This has included sacrificing things that are regarded as precious to us or doing without something that we enjoy. At the extreme limits of this we see self flagellation and even sacrificing children. The result is that the worshippers come to feel that they have made up for any shortcomings they have and at the extreme that God has no choice but to forgive them because they are worth it. This self righteousness can lead to the conclusion that anyone who does not worship the way they do must be stopped. This has led to persecution of religious minorities by the majority population all over the world, a practice that is still prevalent today. At its most extreme in countries like Saudi Arabia there is no tolerance for any religion other than the state sponsored Islam. To get things in balance it must be recognized that it is not only religious groups that show intolerance. The communist atheistic regimes of the USSR, China and North Korea persecuted all religions in their determination to stamp out belief in God.

So what does this have to do with true Bible Christianity? In my opinion nothing at all. We must first acknowledge that at various times "Christendom" has persecuted minorities, encouraged followers to pay penance for their sins and looked the other way while members indulged in all sorts of atrocities. It is my contention that these actions were all undertaken by people who either completely misunderstood the teaching of Jesus or who were cynically only using the title "Christian" to cover their selfish activities. Consider the TV evangelist who offers to pray for sick viewers who send in a donation. One such man claims to pray over a cloth and send it to viewers if they make a suggested contribution. In one case the suggested amount was $1000. To anyone who thinks about the ministry of Jesus this is an atrocious moneymaking scam, aimed at vulnerable, sick people. Jesus never charged to heal and he never failed in an attempt to heal. Any "faith healers" who do not meet these two criteria should be viewed with suspicion.

So let us look at how true Christians should behave compared to the religious behavior we have noted.

Firstly Jesus died for our sins having lived a sin free life. This enabled God to pardon those who genuinely repent of their sins and ask for forgiveness because the punishment they deserved has been fully paid. The Bible says: "No condemnation now hangs over the head of those who are 'in' Christ. For the new spiritual principle of life 'in' Christ lifts me out of the old vicious circle of sin and death."[1] In the words of Jesus: "For God loved the world so much that he gave his only Son, so that anyone who believes on him should not be lost but should have eternal life."[2] Anyone who believes this has no reason to feel themselves superior to any other person. They are in the position of the drowning man who is plucked from the sea by a helicopter rescue crew. They got themselves into the mess and he has lifted them out. There is no need then for any form of sacrifice on their part and penance has no point. This is expressed in the words of the hymn "he has paid it all, all to him I owe." There is nothing we can do to add to our salvation, it is freely offered and fully paid for. Why then do people resist the free offer of salvation? Jesus goes on to say: "Light has entered the world and men have preferred darkness to light because their deeds are evil."[3]

How should we view people who do not believe? Jesus said: "I am the way the truth and the life. No man comes to the Father except through me."[4] That's pretty narrow minded you would say, and if it is the only way, are we justified in forcing people to accept it? The answer must be no. Peter, who spent three years learning from Jesus, said "Never pay back a bad turn with a bad turn or an insult with another insult, but on the contrary pay back with good."[5] Then again Jesus said "love your enemies, and pray for those who persecute you."[6] The message of Christianity is that any of the criticisms leveled against religion by atheists that suggest selfish or bizarre behavior should not apply to the true Christian who can be joyful in the knowledge that they are saved whilst recognizing that it is a free gift and must not result in self righteous pomposity.

Atheists sometimes portray the Apostle Paul as a misogynist, but he was able to write the following words at a time when many cultures and religions regarded women as second class citizens. "For now that you have faith in Christ you are all sons of God. All of you who were baptized 'into' Christ have put on the family likeness of Christ. Gone is the distinction between Jew and Greek, slave and free man, male and female–you are all one in Christ Jesus."[7]

The atheist's desire to replace the blind dogma and hatred found in many religions is understandable, but when they oppose true Christianity with its aims of selfless service to the standards set by God it results in the worship of self. When belief in God is suppressed our spirit retains the desire to commune with and to worship God, so we replace God with celebrities, or things, or self worship. We see the result in western nations as people do what seems right in their own eyes with the result that standards of honesty fall and there is little respect for life itself. Young people taught that they are the result of blind chance believe that there are no absolute standards, leaving them to choose the values they should live by. Not surprisingly they often choose the debased values they see in the lives of the celebrities worshipped by popular culture.

There is no place for hatred towards any group of people in true Christianity, even when we strongly disapprove of how they behave or what they stand for. The Christian will, however, continue to point everyone to the better way seen in the life and teachings of Jesus Christ.

Chapter 9

What's Next?

The purpose of this book is to present the reader with the teachings of Jesus and to show that the known facts about the universe strongly suggest that it was actively created with mankind in mind. Most importantly, however, it is intended to show what this means for you. The first important fact is that Jesus lived a life that was unique because it was without sin. This is very important. If a man or woman wishes to offer themselves to take the punishment that another deserves, they cannot do so if they are serving a sentence for the same crime. Secondly, Jesus said that he would be crucified and that he was doing it for your sins and for mine, so that we have the possibility of not being held to account for our sins. Now we are well aware that many people are not held accountable for their misdeeds. They hire a clever lawyer who gets them off, or the authorities cannot find sufficient evidence to convict them although they are guilty. We call these events miscarriages of justice and we accept them, often with some alarm and annoyance, because we know the system is not perfect. Still other criminals escape justice because they bribe the judge or threaten the jurors or use their political position to suppress incriminating evidence. These cases are due to corruption in the system, not just imperfection. God is neither imperfect nor corrupt. If he has set a punishment for a crime, that punishment must be paid or he is no longer just. By choosing to take the punishment, Jesus, a member of the Holy Trinity, enabled God to be just and the penalty was paid, whilst he dramatically demonstrated his love for us. To take advantage of this free pardon we have to take some action. We need to acknowledge that we are sinners. For most people this should be easy because we know we have done things that are below even our own standards of goodness. Of course today we have experts telling convicted criminals to blame someone else for their problems. It can be their parents or their heritage to blame; they were brought up in a poor environment so antisocial behavior is to be expected or their parents were rich and spoiled them so they never had a chance to behave normally. These excuses fly in the face of the large number of people with similar backgrounds who have overcome them, but this outlook has served to remove the sense of wrongdoing from many people, who have an "I'm OK you're OK" philosophy.

God expects you to make a rational decision now to put away your past, that he will forgive, then make a positive decision to follow him in the future. The people who think that they are perfect, or that their wrong doings are not their fault, clearly find no need for the gospel, but like the speeding motorist who does not believe in speed limits, they will find that they will be forced to pay. Having acknowledged our sins, we must have a desire to be free from them. This of course is the main decision point for many people; they have no wish to be free of their sins. I remember one group of people I worked with who lived for Saturday night when they would go out and get drunk. Their stories of driving home as slowly as possible because they were not in control of themselves and waking up the next morning with severe hangovers painted a picture, for me, of just about the least attractive way I could think of to spend an evening, but they regarded it as the high point of their week. However, we all find some sin attractive and must face up to whether we really want to give it up. On the other hand, some Christian groups have demonized whole areas of pleasure, making the faith seem to amount to a list of things not to do. So what does God want us to strive for? Jesus said the law can be summarized as: "Love the Lord your God with all your heart and with all your soul and with all your mind" and "love your neighbor as yourself."[1] Now these are almost impossible goals but are they desirable? Loving a God who has done so much for us and is now preparing a place in heaven for us should be possible even if the "with all our heart" part is difficult, but Jesus made it clear that whilst the forgiveness of sins is the first step, establishing a loving relationship with him is the intended goal. This love for him comes when we realize the price Jesus paid for our salvation. The apostle John expressed this idea in the words "We love *him*, because he first loved us,"[2] The life of obedience to his word that includes the difficult task of loving others should flow out of this love we have for him. We will always be liable to fail because we are still human but when we fail and confess he is ready to forgive us and restore us. The attitude of God to us when we fail is summed up by Isaiah as: "I have swept away your offenses like a cloud, your sins like a morning mist. Return to me for I have redeemed you."[3]

Think what a world it would be if you could trust any stranger you met. If you could have no locks on the doors, if those with plenty willingly gave enough to make sure everyone was fed and clothed and in reasonable housing. Of course all people would have to ensure they contributed what they could and did not take advantage of the goodness of others, to do nothing. Ideal conditions will exist in heaven and the Christian should be preparing himself as far as possible for this, without being foolish in supporting people who would take advantage of their goodness. If having read to this point you believe the lifestyle that Jesus set before us is the best possible course for your life you may doubt that you are good enough to achieve it. You are right to have such doubts, but Jesus made it clear that he came to save sinners, not those who believe in their own self-righteousness. The good news is that when you accept Jesus as your savior and lord you will get the assistance of God's Holy Spirit to help guide you in your new life. You also have no need to feel worthless because you have failed, God loves you!

If this is what you desire, take the time to pray to God the father in the name of Jesus. Tell him you know that you are a sinner and that you realize that Jesus died to pay the penalty for your sin. Express your desire to live a life in accordance with God's will for you and ask for forgiveness. Ask for the guidance of the Holy Spirit in your life and resolve to read the New Testament, starting with the Gospel of John or Luke. Find a church where this simple Gospel is preached and make sure no one talks you into believing you need to do anything else to be saved. It is clear that the early Christians got baptized and had a simple meal of bread and wine to remember the Lord Jesus and that he had shed his blood for them. These things should be practiced in the church you choose, but this is not part of salvation. Salvation is a free gift given by the grace of God to those who accept it by faith.

Those who accept the words of Jesus can look forward positively to a bright future, nonbelievers see only a pointless existence. Both Jesus[4] and scientists predict the end of the earth. Weinberg says the universe faces "a future extinction of endless cold or intolerable heat" and he concludes that "The effort to understand the universe is one of the few things that lifts human life a little above the level of farce, and gives it some of the grace of tragedy."[5] A more recent prediction of science is that the Universe will expand at an ever increasing rate until it tears itself apart. No wonder so many atheists are depressed and turn to alcohol and drugs. If we are just a collection of chemicals put together in such a way as to ensure the survival of our genes how can we be sure that any of our abstract thoughts have any relevance whatsoever? The logic that we have used to deduce scientific theorems may be completely flawed. The early scientists such as Newton worked with the certainty that a rational God was behind creation and on this basis he did his research. The atheist is trusting that chance combinations of chemicals in his brain have produced legitimate results when he could be deceiving himself about their validity. The Christian chemist Professor Humphries says "For me God is the necessary undergirding of all our work as scientists, for without Him as sufficient cause the fundamental rational for all we observe is gone and we are left without any ultimate meaning."[6] Jesus said "It is true that I am going away to prepare a place for you, but it is just as true that I am coming again to welcome you into my own home."[7] Christians should be the most joyful people on earth.

I will close with words from Paul, firstly as he closed his letter to the Philippians "...If you believe in goodness and if you value the approval of God, fix your minds on the things which are holy and right and pure and beautiful and good."[8] Secondly, from his letter to the Thessalonians "Be happy in your faith at all times. Never stop praying. Be thankful whatever the circumstances may be."[9]

References

Chapter 1

1) Antiquities of the Jews xviii 3.3 Josephus

2) The New Testament Documents are they Reliable F F Bruce Intervarsity Press 5th Edition Chapter 9. Page 103

3) Annals Book 15 Chapter 44 Tacitus

4) The New Testament Documents are they Reliable F.F. Bruce Intervarsity Press 5th Edition Chapter 2. Page11

5) Paul's first letter to the Corinthians Chapter15 vs 6 J.B.Phillips. The New Testament in Modern English Bles Collins 1959

6) Letter from Clement of Rome to Church at Corinth.(See www.newadvent.org)

7) Acts Chapter 26 vs 8–22

8) John Chapter 3 vs 16. J.B.Phillips. op.cit.

9) Paul's letter to the Romans Chapter 3   vs 23,24. J.B.Phillips. op.cit.

10) 2 Peter Chapter 3 vs 15

11) Luke Chapter 3 vs 1,2. J.B.Phillips. op.cit.

12) Luke Chapter1 vs 1–4 J.B.Phillips. op.cit.

13) Colossians Chapter 4 vs 10,14

14) The New Testament Documents are they Reliable F F Bruce Intervarsity Press 5th Edition Chapter 4. Pages 32,33

15) Acts Chapter 13 vs 7. J.B.Phillips. op.cit.

16) The New Testament Documents are they Reliable F F Bruce. Intervarsity Press 5th Edition Chapter 7. Page 83

17) The Bearing of Recent Discovery on the trustworthiness of the New Testament. Sir William Ramsey 1915. Page 89

18) Acts Chapter 23 vs 26

19) The Books and the Parchments F F Bruce 1950

Pickering & Inglis. Page 182

20) The Books and the Parchments F F Bruce 1950

Pickering & Inglis. Page 179

21) The Bible and Archeology F G Kenyon 1940

Harper & Row New York. Pages 288-89

Chapter 2

1) John Chapter 11 Vs 38 to 45.

2) Psalm Chapter 8 Vs 3,4.

3) Natural Theology on Evidence and Attributes of Deity. W. Paley 1807 Faulder & Son

4) The Origin of the Species. C.Darwin. John Murray 1876 6ᵗʰ Edition. Page 429

5) The Science of God. G.L.Schroeder Broadway Books 1997. Page38,39

6) Darwin's Black Box. Michael Behe.1996 The Free Press

7) Mere Christianity. C.S.Lewis.2001 Harper Collins. Chapter1. Page 10

8) BBC Newsnight 1st June 2007

9) Gladys Aylward. The Little Woman. Gladys Aylward and Christine Hunter Moody Publishers U.S. 1970

10) Robber of the Cruel Streets. Clive Langmead. CWR Waverley 2006

11) Divine Guidance. G.H.Lang.1947

12) Stories from around the World. Keith Danby (Editor) Authentic Media 2005

13) The Cross and the switchblade. David Wilkerson Penguin Putnam October 1977

14) Once an Arafat Man.Tass Saada Tyndale House 2008

Chapter 3

1) John Chapter 14 vs 9 New King James. Thomas Nelson 1989

2) John Chapter 10 vs 30 New King James. Thomas Nelson 1989

3) Mere Christianity C.S. Lewis. HarperCollins 2001 Chapter 3. Page 52

4) John Chapter 14 vs 6 New King James. Thomas Nelson 1989

5) John Chapter 15 vs 20,21

6) Mark Chapter 14 vs 61-64

7) Luke Chapter 3 vs 7 New King James. Thomas Nelson 1989

8) Matthew Chapter 5 vs 21-44 New King James. Thomas Nelson 1989

9) Matthew Chapter 4 vs 23,24

10) Luke Chapter 7 vs 1-10

11) John Chapter 9 vs 1-9

12) Mark Chapter 10 vs 35-45

13) John Chapter 20 vs 24-28

14) Matt Chapter 14 vs 22-36

15) Mark Chapter 8 vs 33

16) Mark Chapter 14 vs 66-72

17) Luke Chapter 15 vs 12-32

18) Leviticus Chapter 4 vs 8

19) Isaiah Chapter 53 vs 5 New International Bible Zondervan Publishers Michigan 1989

20) John Chapter 4 vs 25,26

21) John Chapter 3 vs 16-19 J.B.Phillips. The New Testament in Modern English Bles Collins 1959

22) Matthew Chapter 22 vs 13

23) John Chapter 14 vs 2

24) Luke Chapter 24 vs 13-31 J.B.Phillips. op.cit.

25) John Chapter 21 vs 3

26) John Chapter 7 vs 5

27) 1Corinthians Chapter 15 vs 7

28) Galatians Chapter 1 vs 13

29) Acts Chapter 7 vs 58

30) Acts Chapter 26 vs 9-20

31) Luke Chapter 6:29

See also "Who Moved the Stone." Frank Morison Faber and Faber

Chapter 4

1) Psalm 14:Vs 1. The New King James Bible. Thomas Nelson 1989.

2) Psalm 53 Vs 1. The New King James Bible. Thomas Nelson 1989.

3) The Origin Of the Species. C. Darwin. John Murray 1876. 6th Edition. Page 429.

4) Psalm 19 Vs 1. The New International Bible. Zondervan 1988.

5) The First Three Minutes. Steven Weinberg. Basic Books New York 1977. Page 154

6) God and the New Physics. Paul Davies. Simon & Schuster New York Touchstone Edition 1984. Page 179.

7)The First Three Minutes. Steven Weinberg. Basic Books New York 1977. Page 8

8) The Emperor's New Mind. Roger Penrose. Oxford University Press 1989. Page 444.

9) A Brief History of Time. Stephen Hawking. Bantam Books London 1988.

10) The Elegant Universe. Brian Greene. Vintage Books New York 2000. Page 13.

11) Nature's Destiny. Michael Denton. The Free Press London 1998.

12) The Universe Plan or Accident. R.E.D.Clark. Paternoster Press London.

13) Nature's Destiny. Michael Denton. Op.cit. pp 32-38

14) Modern Valency Theory. G.I.Brown. Longmans Green & Co. Page 80

15) Nature's Destiny. Michael Denton. Op.cit. pp 203,204

16) Introduction to the Chemistry of Life. P.B.Berlow,D.J.Berton,J.I.Routh. Saunders College Publishing 1982. Pages 598-602

17) Nature's Destiny. Michael Denton. Op.cit. Page 121

18) Encyclopedia Britannica 2005. Photosynthesis.

19) Nature's Destiny. Michael Denton. Op.cit. P 55

20)Nature's Destiny. Michael Denton. Op.cit. P 53

21) The Emperor's New Mind. Roger Penrose. Oxford University Press 1989. Page 414.

22) The Blind Watchmaker. Richard Dawkins. W W Norton New York 1996. Page 41

Chapter 5

1) The Origin of the Species. Charles Darwin. John Murray 1876. 6th Edition

2) New ideas from dead economists. Todd G.Buchho. Penguin Books London 1999. Page 49

3) Evolution a theory in Crisis. Michael Denton.Adler & Adler Maryland 1996. Page 79

4) Evolution a theory in Crisis; Michael Denton. Adler & Adler Maryland 1996. Page 50

5) Evolution a theory in Crisis; Michael Denton. Adler & Adler Maryland 1996. Page 161

6) The Science of God. Gerald L.Schroeder. Broadway Books NewYork 1997. Page 34

7) Reinventing Darwin. Niles Eldridge. Wiley New York 1995. Page 95

8) The Richness of Life. Stephen Jay Gould. Vintage Books London 2007. Page 6

9) Lecture at Hobart & William Smith College, Feb 14 1980; Stephen Jay Gould

10) Development of Avian Respiratory and Circulation Systems; H.R. Duncker ed J Piiper Springer Verlag 1978
New York. Pages 260-273

11) Nature's Destiny. Michael Denton. The Free Press London 1998. Page 362

12) Nature's Destiny. Michael Denton. The Free Press London 1998. Page 362-363

13) The Emperor's New Mind. Roger Penrose. Oxford University Press 1989. Page 535

14) The Hidden face of God. Gerald L.Schroeder. Simon & Schuster New York 2001. Page 58

15) Microbiology Demystified. Tom Betsy and Jim Keogh. McGraw Hill New York 2005. Page 68

16) J. Horgan. "Profile Francis H.C.Crick." Scientific American. October 1994

17) The Language of God. Francis S. Collins. Free Press New York 2006. Page 124

18) The Science of God. Gerald L.Schroeder. Broadway Books NewYork 1997. Pages102-104

19) Energy Flow in Biology. Harold J. Morovitz. Ox Bow Press 1979. Page 67

20) The Blind Watchmaker. Richard Dawkins. W W Norton New York 1996. Page 46

21) The Hidden face of God. Gerald L.Schroeder.Simon & Schuster New York 2001. Page100

22) Darwin's Black Box; Michael Behe. The Free Press. 1996

23) Logic Design Algorithms. D.Zissos. Oxford University Press. 1972

24) The Richness of Life. Stephen Jay Gould. Vintage Books London 2007. Page 147

25) Evolution a theory in Crisis. Michael Denton.Adler & Adler Maryland 1996. Page 209

26) Mutations from "Evolution". Encyclopedia Britannica 2005.

27) The Blind Watchmaker. Richard Dawkins. W W Norton New York 1996

28) The Language of God. Francis S. Collins. Free Press New York 2006. Page 200

29) Evolution or Creation. H. Enoch. Evangelical Press London November 1966

30) "Supernova" From Encyclopedia Britannica 2005.

31) "Heredity" From Encyclopedia Britannica 2005.

32) The Language of God. Francis S. Collins. Free Press New York 2006. Page 124

33) The Science of God. Gerald L.Schroeder. Broadway Books NewYork 1997. Page 93

34) Statistical Methods. Donald L. Harnett. Addison-Wesley 1982. Page 79

Chapter 6

1) Relativity by Einstein. Albert Einstein. Tess Press. New York. Page134

2) Einstein's Cosmos. Michio Kaku. Pheonix. London 2005. Page101

3) The First Three Minutes. Steven Weinberg. Basic Books. New York 1977. Pages 15-21

4) The Hidden face of God. Gerald L.Schroeder. Simon & Schuster. New York 2001. Page 45

5) The First Three Minutes. Steven Weinberg. Basic Books New York 1977. Page 154

6) The Science of God. Gerald L.Schroeder. Broadway Books NewYork 1997. Page 17

7) Berezhis-Rashi commentary. Book1 Genesis

8) John Chapter 1 vs 1-5

9) The First Three Minutes. Steven Weinberg. Basic Books New York 1977. Page 30

10) Genesis and the Big Bang. Gerald L.Schroeder. Bantam Books 1992. Pages 96,97

11) Leviticus chapter 23 verse 32

12) Microbiology Demystified. Tom Betsy and Jim Keogh. McGraw Hill New York 2005.. Page174

13) Elso Barghoorn. Minnesota State University E-museum

14) The Science of God. Gerald L.Schroeder. Broadway Books NewYork 1997. Pages 90,91

15) The Science of God. Gerald L.Schroeder. Broadway Books NewYork 1997. Page 17

16) Science Speaks. Peter W Stoner. Moody Press Chicago 1958. Page 47

17) The Language of God. Francis S. Collins. Free Press New York 2006. Page 152

18) Psalm 90 verse 4

19) The Molecules we are made of Dr. David A. Humphreys

20) Creation, Evolution and Intelligent Design. Professor Sir Brian Heap. Perspectives Number 43 Winter 2010 Partnership Books, Paternoster Press.

Old Testament quotations are from the Authorized King James translation, Oxford University Press and
The New King James translation Thomas Nelson Publishers.

Chapter 7

1) Genesis Chapter 1 vs 28
2) St Augustus. Enchridion xi.
3) The Problem of Pain. C.S. Lewis. Fontana Books 1961. Page 81
4) Jeremiah Chapter 18 vs 1-10
5) The Return of Depression Economics. Paul Krugman W.W.Norton & Company. New York. 2009. Page 165.
6) Hebrews Chapter 13 vs 5
7) Isaiah Chapter 53 vs 4 New International Bible Zondervan Publishers Michigan 1989
8) Matthew Chapter 23 vs 37 J.B.Phillips. The New Testament in Modern English Bles Collins 1959
9) The Problem of Pain. C.S. Lewis. Fontana Books 1961. Page 3
10) Genesis 18; 18
11) Psalms Chapter 23 vs 1 New International Bible Zondervan Publishers Michigan 1989 .

Chapter 8

1) Romans Chapter 8 vs 1,2 J.B.Phillips. The New Testament in Modern English Bles Collins 1959
2) John Chapter 3 vs 16 Phillips op.cit.
3) John Chapter 3 vs 19 Phillips op.cit.
4) John Chapter 14 vs 6 The New King James translation Thomas Nelson Publishers.
5) 1 Peter Chapter 3 vs 9 Phillips op.cit.
6) Matthew Chapter 5 vs 44 Phillips op.cit.

7) Galatians Chapter 3 vs 27,28 Phillips op.cit.

Chapter 9

1) Matthew Chapter 22 vs 37-41. New International Bible
Zondervan Publishers Michigan 1989

2) 1John Chapter 4 vs 19. New International Bible

3) Isaiah Chapter 44 vs 22. New International Bible Zondervan
Publishers Michigan 1989

4) Matthew Chapter 28 vs20

5) The First Three Minutes. Steven Weinberg. Basic Books New York
1977. Pages 154,155

6) Relating science and faith. Dr. David A.Humphreys. Frontiers of
Science and Chrisianity. Divinity College

7) John Chapter14 vs 3. J.B.Phillips. The New Testament in Modern
English Bles Collins 1959

8) Philippians Chapter 4 vs 8,9. J.B.Phillips. op.cit.

9) 1 Thessalonians Chapter 5 vs 16-18. J.B.Phillips. op.cit.

Made in the USA
Charleston, SC
29 October 2014